Finding Your Way Back
to the
Straight and Narrow Path

A Jack Mormon's Travel Guide

Finding Your Way Back
— to the —
Straight and Narrow Path

By
GM Jarrard

Capitol Ideas Publishing
South Jordan, Utah

Published in 2006 by Capitol Ideas Publishing
PO Box 95274 • South Jordan, Utah 84095-0275
(801) 599-4858

ISBN — 0-9711407-7-4

Printed and bound in the United States of America by *PrintJobs*, Ogden, Utah

10 9 8 7 6 5 4 3 2 1

To my mother, Edna Littlefield Jarrard, who like so many wives and mothers (and fathers) had the faith, patience and endurance to help their loved ones leave the wilderness of inactivity and return to the Straight and Narrow Path.

SPECIAL THANKS ...

To my wife, Christie, for hearing me talk about this book for years before I did anything about it and who has supported me in everything I have ever done, including doing some proofreading herself.

To my colleague Joe Bonyata who proofread the book and caught more mistakes than I care to admit.

To editor, publisher and former co-worker Cord Udall who helped publish the title.

To my printer and friend Todd Tenney of PrintJobs who delivered the final product.

And to long-time friend and colleague Bruce Hough who helped expedite the printing.

Finally, to my father, Jack E. Jarrard, whose willingness to change his life was the inspiration for this book.

Contents —

Preface

I struggled with the title of this book. By nature, I am a person who enjoys a laugh – I see whimsy in many situations. There are times to be serious, but I never take myself too seriously. I have my father to thank for that.

He is the inspiration for this book. Before he died in March of 2001, I told him I was working on a story about activation, about coming back to church and taking your family to the temple. I said he played a big part in it; in fact, he was a main character. What's it called, he asked? "The Confessions of a Jack Mormon's Son, or "So You Want to Be a Jack Mormon." What?!! He shouted at me. (You needed to know my dad; he was kind of a Mormon version of Walter Matthau, even after he became "active.") "I was never a Jack Mormon," he groused.

Then my mother joined the conversation:

"Yes, you were," she said matter-of-factly. "You smoked, you drank, you didn't come to church. I took the kids to church and you stayed home ... for awhile until you had a change of heart and decided to change."

After some grumbling, the subject turned to dinner and I decided not to pursue the title of my impending book at that time.

Truth be told, my father's change of heart took major surgery. He was asked in the summer of 1957 if he wanted to ordain his son, me, a deacon. He replied he would like to but he didn't consider himself worthy. Bishop Jeppson smiled.

"That's why we're having this conversation," he said, "... to get you worthy."

In Dad's case, it was smoking. He thought it was a secret by this time. He had been serving as the Sunday School teacher for my age group, and the boys knew about his secret habit and reminded me of it regularly. Most of them had a nickname: there was Spider, Beak and Guppy. Since my dad's name was Jack, and he was, by definition, a Jack Mormon, that became my handle: Jack Mormon. I don't think I was a Jack Mormon at the age of 11; nevertheless, it was a name that stuck with me for several years, even after my dad underwent ulcer surgery (as he went cold turkey and swore off tobacco). So at Scout camps and at various activities for several years, that was my nickname long after our family went to the temple and were sealed together.

That's the funny thing about labels: They are often misleading and can do a disservice to the people who wear them. But looking back, I now think of that label with some pride because of what it means to me: My father made changes in his life because he loved his family and because he wanted to ordain me a deacon. The picture of being brought into the sealing room at the Salt Lake Temple with my brother and sisters and seeing my parents and grand-mothers waiting for us there is engraven in my mind's eye. For me, that was a life-altering event; my mother's patience and devotion had paid off. Our family was an eternal unit. Now it was up to us to be true and faithful to earn those promised blessings.

Historically, the name "Jack Mormon" was applied by enemies of the church to the non-Mormon friends of the saints who gave them aid and comfort. To those anti-Mormons, both "Mormon" and "Jack Mormon" were terms of derision. Later, the term began known as inactive LDS members who showed up now and then and cooked flapjacks at ward breakfasts but who could be spotted with a cup of coffee at the local diner any other day of the week. As a young bishop, however, I took it to mean members who would gladly join if they knew they were loved and welcome, and if someone would help them overcome their problems and show them the way.

It is for them this book is written.

Chapter One — Smoke & Mirrors

Anyone who grew up in the 1950s and had a radio or TV is familiar with the phrase, "Lucky Strike Means Fine Tobacco." Even at the age of 9, I was. At the time, we were living on Layton Avenue west of Main Street in Salt Lake City. It was early evening, and my dad and I were relaxing – watching our old 12-inch, black-and-white Motorola.

"Greg, go get me my sheroots, will ya'?" he asked, pointing at his pack of Luckies on the dining room table. I obeyed, and as he sat back in his easy chair to enjoy that fine tobacco I snuggled up on his lap. I put my arms around his neck and made him a promise:

"When I grow up I'm going to smoke Lucky Strikes just like you, Dad!" I declared.

Suddenly out of the kitchen came a flash, a whirling dervish, black eyes a' flashing. It was my mother, all 5'2" of her towering over both of us.

"See, see what kind of example you're setting for that boy! Luckies? Luckies?! It's not bad enough that you smoke in the house with him in your lap, now he's decided he's going to join you. Why not just give him one now and let him light up?!"

This was over 50 years ago. Today, my mother can't clearly remember the incident (she admits maybe she overreacted). But for me, it was a turning point. Since that time, I have not rendered a brand preference for tobacco products of any kind. The talk that followed also helped me decide that sheroots weren't for me.

"You know, son," my dad explained, "your mom's right. Smoking's not a good thing. I'd like to quit."

"Well, why don't you?"

" I have — quite a few times. It's not that easy. I want you to make me a promise — that you'll never start. Will you promise me that?"

"Yes sir, I will," I said.

There is a happy ending to all of this. Three or four years later, Dad did quit and changed his life in many other ways. His quitting put him in the hospital with a perforated ulcer and cost him part of his small intestine. After surgery, he couldn't stand the smell of tobacco. He became tobacco's archenemy. That's why years later when I was serving as a young bishop, his advice to me sounded strange at first:

"You know, son, there's nothing that smells better than tobacco in church."

"What?" I asked.

"The smell of a smoker sitting in the last row during a sacrament meeting. Some might turn up their noses at the lingering scent of tobacco on a visitor's clothes, but when it's in church, it's a wonderful aroma," he said. "Because it means that someone wants to change, someone wants to turn their life around. When you sense that, jump on it. Make those people feel welcome.

"The thing about smoking is, it's hard to hide," he continued. "You can't smell dishonesty or infidelity, guile or cruelty or most other vices. So, from that standpoint, smoking is just a small obstacle compared to others."

He was right. On the road to the Straight and Narrow Path, there are all kinds of stumbling blocks. Sometimes we trip over them, sometimes we take a detour. Too often, they stop us in our tracks. That's what tobacco is: a stumbling block, not a wall. On the Straight and Narrow Path, there aren't any dead ends.

But there are gates we have to unlock.

A couple of years ago, we made the trek to Gettysburg, a place I had always wanted to see. At the visitors center, we viewed the site map. On it were three words: "You Are Here." It made me pause. I thought, how do they know where I am? The point is, *where you are now* is your starting place. The important thing isn't where you've been. What's important is to be on the path. Somewhere on his journey, my dad came to the realization that he wasn't on the path.

Sometimes it takes a child to point that out and force some serious self-examination. During the "Lucky Strike" period, I would occasionally accompany my dad to work on Saturday mornings. He was an editor at the Deseret News at the time, and Saturday mornings gave him some time to organize his work for the week, and I think, avoid unpleasant chores at home. At any rate, we would go in about 9:30 or 10:00 a.m., shuffle some papers and then by noon make the exciting journey through the alley behind Richards Street and sneak in the back door of the Duncan Café.

It was in the Duncan Café that I had my first malt. It was a caramel malt in a tall glass accompanied by a cold, stainless steel canister with more of the sweet, frothy elixir. The glass was so tall in fact that I had to get on my knees to reach the straw. That's when I remembered: We hadn't said a blessing on the food! We were in the booth with two of my dad's friend, two hard-bitten reporters, both World War II vets.

"Do you want me to say a blessing on the food?" I asked.

Dad glanced at his friends, who looked away and bit their lips.

"See Cookie back there behind those swinging doors?" he asked.

"The sailor guy?" I responded, catching a glimpse of a tough old Navy cook in a T-shirt and apron, a pack of sheroots tucked into his shirtsleeve just above a large tattoo.

"Yeah, the sailor guy," Dad continued. "He's the cook." Dad paused for effect. "Anyway, every morning before he comes to work, before any customers come in and order their breakfast, do you know what he does?"

"No," I answered truthfully.

"He takes a moment, bows his head and says a blessing on all the food that all the people will eat in this restaurant that day."

"Really?"

"Really."

That was good enough for me. The malt was delicious. In fact, it tasted absolutely blessed! I believed for years that cooks all over America did the same thing: removed their sailor caps, folded their thick tattooed arms, bowed their heads and blessed the food at the beginning of each day. I believe now that little episode served a purpose: It gave my dad pause — food for thought. Children instinctively believe what their parents tell them to be true. And, children can often be teachers. When he made his ultimate decision to quit smoking and go to the temple it was because a good bishop challenged him to become worthy to ordain his son — me — a deacon.

It had been a long journey, but at the age of 41, Dad was on the path.

In Ecclesiastes, we read that for every thing there is a season, a time to laugh, a time to cry, a time to be born and a time to die. I also believe if we take a long hard look in the mirror, we can see that there are times to change our lives — opportunities to get back on the path. The Lord not only has a general plan of salvation for mankind, I believe He also has a specific plan for each of His children because He is a successful parent, one not bound by time, events or place.

Sometimes we face major events in our lives that require us to make changes. These are often great opportunities to get on the path. Ask yourself these questions:

- Is there a baby on the way?
- How about a wedding? Yours? A child's?
- Is there a crisis in your marriage? Divorce?
- Health problems?
- Has there been a death in the family? Have you lost someone close to you?
- Do you have a child turning 8? A son turning 12 — or 19?
- Have you lost your job?
- Are you moving, getting transferred?

Some of these events are painful, others are joyous. They are all times of reflection when we pause and examine the direction our lives have taken and then redirect our journey. If we have missed a turnoff and taken an unplanned detour, it's a chance to look at the map. Take a moment and look at the place where it says, "You Are Here."

That's where your new journey begins.

Chapter Two — Getting from Here to There

You are here for a reason. And, it's to be tested. The scriptures tell us that we were sent to Earth, in the Lord's words, "to prove them herewith to see if they will do all things whatsoever the Lord their God shall command them."

"This life is just a test," a bumper sticker stated, "if it had been a real life there would have been instructions." The writer who penned those words didn't realize that there are, in fact, detailed instructions: the scriptures. And one thing the scriptures tell us is that there IS a purpose for our being here. As we read in the Book of Mormon, "Adam fell that man might be, and men are that they might have joy."

So, you are here to have joy — and to be tested. And, the scriptures provide us with a map so we can enjoy the trip.

During our family's Jack Mormon years, we had an old green 1948 Dodge four-door sedan. On most Sunday nights, we would visit one of my grandmas or my uncle and aunt in Bountiful. After an evening of adult conversation and a treat, we would climb in the old Dodge for the ride home. It was wide enough that my sister Jeannie and I could stretch out in the backseat. We would watch as shadows of street lamps danced around inside the darkened car like ghosts in an eerie game of hide and seek. We would curl up and hide our eyes and then fall asleep. Someone would carry us into our beds because in the morning that's where we would find ourselves.

One night, however, it was different. I remember snuggling on the backseat of a moving car and awakening much later and finding myself all alone. I peered over the back of the front seat and to my horror, no one was driving — and no one was in the front seat! The old green Dodge, however, was traveling down a dark country road with huge trees on one side and a barbed-wire fence on the other. The headlights threw out two long cones of light, but there was nothing to see but the country road, poplars and the fence line. I was helpless in the backseat. I curled back up on the seat and closed my eyes. The next thing I knew, it was morning — I was back to reality. It had been a bad dream of being abandoned in the backseat, headed for a destination over which I had no control. What's interesting is that

I had this dream repeatedly over the years and never knew what it meant.

Years later, I was sitting on the stand in sacrament meeting as a young bishop presiding over a new ward. We had real challenges — more families headed by inactive parents than active families led by Melchizedek priesthood holders. Dozens of children sat home every Sunday, never to be taken to church and never to be taught precious Gospel principles. Then it hit me: They were confined to the backseat of a car with no one at the wheel. They were headed in an uncertain direction. They were in spiritual danger!

Then, family by family, we began meeting with these parents and their precious passengers. When we were allowed, we sent home teachers. When they responded, lessons were taught and goals were set. Within a few years, a dozen new families tasted the Gospel fruit. Drivers were found for the family sedans. And destinations were changed. One by one, husbands and wives learned their purpose as parents — to teach their children about faith, repentance, baptism and the Gift of the Holy Ghost and how the Gospel is God's Plan of Happiness for their children.

"Happiness" is an overused word. Is happiness the same as pleasure? Is it synonymous with joy? What makes people really happy? Is happiness...

- having a great job and making a lot of money?

- buying countless toys to stuff in your garage?

- engaging in stimulating activities, rock climbing, sky diving and other extreme sports?

- seeing the world, traveling constantly and dining in exotic places?

- raising a beautiful family, living in palatial sur-roundings?

In the end, isn't happiness the endgame of human existence, our reason for being? Then, how do we get there? And how do we separate those things that mere-ly give us pleasure from those that deliver true joy? The truth is, the things listed here all come at a cost — there's always a trade-off. You can't really engage in a lifetime of travel and extreme outdoor activities AND raise a large family and be there for your children. Pres. David O. McKay put it best when he said, **"No other success can compensate for failure in the home."** It's easy to deceive ourselves, to think all is well as our children slip through our fingers. We need to ask ourselves the question, **"what matters most?"** (stealing a phrase from a time-management company).

To answer that question, it's important to remember that life really is a journey. And with children, it's more like a long, extended family vacation. It's a trip that requires a road map — provided to us by the Gospel — that shows why we're here, where we've been and where we're going. I don't know about you, but a family vacation can sometimes skirt with disaster. One trip our family went on was no exception.

We began in Oceanside, Calif., at a beachfront condo. I should have left well enough alone. But I had heard that straight east up in the mountains was a site I had always wanted to see ever since I was a nerdy kid studying astronomy. The Mt. Palomar Observatory was somewhere "in them thar' hills" and I wanted to see it. And I wanted to drag my family along with me. We loaded up our giant, ugly orange-and-brown, 7-miles-to-the-gallon Ford van and headed east. It was the last time we had all seven kids under our wings, and as I exaggerated, it was a chance to peer through the eyepiece and maybe catch a glimpse of an alien napping. So off we went.

It was farther — much farther — than I had supposed. Along the way, things caught my attention that distracted me from my goal. Twenty minutes up the road, we came to an orange grove, and I saw those three magic words: "Pick Your Own." I had always wanted my own orange grove, or at least a tree or two (in Utah, my apricots usually freeze!). So, I pulled over and we sent the brood scurrying up ladders and low-lying branches. Soon, we had a couple of sacks of oranges and climbed back in. Sure, it was a delayed detour, I thought, but no problem. We were on the road again!

A little farther up was another distraction. Along the roadside were wild cactuses loaded with prickly pears, a delicacy I learned to eat from street vendors while serving as a missionary in Italy many years before. Again, seven children, ages 2 to 17, piled out, along with my wife, who gave me an all-telling eye-roll that communicates paragraphs and paragraphs. At that moment, I only had prickly pears on my mind. We soon discovered why these pears were called prickly. No sooner were we back in the van than a couple of kids tried eating our newly found treasure, only to discover little white stickers in their lips made painful by prickly pear juice. (It's kind of like getting lemon juice in a paper cut!) Within a few minutes, we were rolling back and forth from the switchbacks with oranges and prickly pears sloshing around on the floor of the van like an orange-brown schooner passing around the Horn. For me and my crew, it was *Mutiny on the Bounty*.

Even the first officer was in on it by now. No one had wanted to see the giant telescope but me. The words, "Are We There Yet?" are forever ingrained in my mind.

No one had wanted to stop and pick oranges and prickly pears but me. And once we had arrived, there wasn't much to see — just a five-minute in-and-out tour (they operate at night, after all!). A childhood dream had become my familiar nightmare, only now I was the one behind the wheel. It was a long trip back to the beach. It was a painful lesson for the driver.

Yes, life with children really is one long road trip — a family vacation that lasts 18 – 20 years or so per passenger. And, we're never there yet. But, lucky for us Latter-day Saints, we have a road map! An eternal perspective to show us the road ahead. We call it the Plan of Salvation. Revealed in these latter days, it gives us a bird's eye view of where we came from, why we are here and where we are going. Let's take a closer look at it.

Chapter Three — Plans or Coincidences?

Ever had a bad day? God knew you would, so He came up with a plan. I believe that not only is there a General Plan of Salvation for all men, but there is also a Specific Plan of Salvation for You. My wife believes there is no such thing as a coincidence when it comes to really important things, and the older I get, the more I believe that is so. God is able to see from the beginning to the end. The scriptures say that all things to Him are one eternal round. The events in our lives happen one moment at a time, in linear fashion. But, God isn't bound by such limitations. C.S. Lewis notes that, to God, we are like characters in a book — beloved characters — that he can put down, bookmark, come back to and pick up where He left off. So, when He sees trouble coming our way, He can make contingency plans, just in case we mess up or get ourselves in a fix (like that flawed character in a book).

And we all mess up, don't we? Even the Prophet Joseph Smith did. It is recorded in the Doctrine and Covenants for all the world to read — and learn from.

Martin Harris, one of the Three Witnesses of the Book of Mormon, had been hounding the Prophet about the manuscript, the first 116 pages of the translation that he wanted to show his wife. Martin believed the Prophet's work; the problem was, his wife didn't. He figured if he showed her the transcript in progress she would be on board. So, he had been hounding the prophet. Martin asked him once, twice and then a third time. Finally, the Lord allowed Joseph to loan him the manuscript. Days later, Martin returned to the Prophet empty-handed, crying all was lost. Devastated, Joseph went to the Lord.

> *...because you have delivered up these writings which you had power given unto you to translate by means of the Urim and Thummim into the hands of a wicked man, you have lost them. And you also lost your gift at the same time, and your mind became darkened.* (D&C 10:1 – 2)

And then the Lord tells the Prophet NOT to retranslate the portion of the large plates designated as the Book of Lehi, but rather to go to the small plates and start over, translating what we now recognize as Ist Nephi. The Lord explains why:

> *Verily, I say unto you, that I will not suffer that Satan shall accomplish his evil design in this thing* [make note of that thought]. *For behold, he has put it into their*

hearts to tempt the Lord, thy God, in asking to translate it over again. (D&C 10:14 – 15)

Centuries earlier, knowing what would happen beforehand, the Lord made preparations. About 600 B.C., the Book of Mormon prophet Nephi was commanded to prepare **two** sets of plates. He didn't understand why and makes this note:

Wherefore, the Lord hath commanded me to make these plates for a wise purpose in him, which purpose I know not. But the Lord knoweth all things from the beginning; wherefore, he prepareth a way to accomplish all his works among the children of men; for behold, he hath all power unto the fulfilling of all his words. And thus it is, Amen. (I Nephi 9:5 – 6)

About 385 A.D., another prophet, Mormon, is commanded by the Lord to include these smaller plates with his record so that when he hands them over to his son, Moroni, they will eventually be buried and hidden up by the Lord until they are delivered to the prophet Joseph some 1,400 years later. Mormon declares:

And I do this for a wise purpose; for thus it whispereth me, according to the workings of the Spirit of the Lord which is in me. And now, I do not know all things; ***but the Lord knoweth all things which are to come;*** *wherefore, he worketh in me to do according to his will."* (Words of Mormon: 7)

During the process of translation, Joseph and Martin took a detour — they strayed from the Straight and Narrow Path. But, since the Lord knew ahead of time that they would, he made contingency plans. Satan, the Devil, Old Scratch — whatever you call him — doesn't enjoy such eternal foresight. That was his undoing, as this passage illustrates:

> *And Satan put it into the heart of the serpent (for he had drawn away man after him), and he sought also to beguile Eve,* **for he knew not the mind of God,** *wherefore he sought to destroy the world.* (Moses 4:6)

Take note of that: He knew not the mind of God! Satan will go to any length to cloud our vision, block our way and get us off track so that we take an uncharted path. But, doesn't the Lord love us just as He loved Joseph and Martin? I would suggest that in your life God does place stepping-stones, trail markers and road signs — and fellow travelers — along the way to help you find your way back knowing you will stumble. You must be wise and humble enough to see them and make use of them.

Never forget what the Lord is all about, what His mission is:

> *For behold, this is my work and my glory — to bring to pass the immortality and eternal life of man.* (Moses 1:39)

The scriptures explain that all of us, each and every soul, is an eternal being who once lived in light and glory before we came to this Earth (see Romans 8:16 – 17, Abraham 3:22 – 28 and Moses 4:1 – 4). There were two plans presented there, one that required us to walk by faith and learn from our experience the difference between good and evil. Jesus Christ was the author of the plan, and those of us who have been privileged enough to come to this Earth accepted it. It called for a Fall (see II Nephi 2: 17 – 18, Moses 3:5, Genesis 2:7 – 8, 2 – 23, II Nephi 2:19 –23, D&C 29:40 – 41) or, in other words, a departure from the presence of God so that we could be tested. And, it said that we would undergo our earthly probation and experience pleasure and pain, joy and misery, sin and repentance and everything else in between (see Alma 34:32, II Nephi 2:27, D&C 93:12 – 14, 19-20 and 29-32). Because we would sin and make ourselves unworthy to return to the presence of God, a savior was prepared to offer Himself as a sacrifice if we would repent and accept His conditions of repentance. To all these things, we agreed.

For as in Adam all die, even so in Christ shall all be made alive. (I Corinthians 15:22). We learn that after death, we are admitted into the Spirit World to continue our probation until the resurrection of the body and the spirit. (see Alma 40:9 – 14, II Nephi 9:10 – 13, I Corinthians 15, I Peter 4:6 and D&C 138). Here the righteous spirits are separated from the unrighteous ones. But, the work of preaching the Gospel and repentance continues. The saving ordinances of the Gospel, however, are performed by proxy here on the Earth for those who accept the preaching on the other side. That is why we have temples.

When the Lord's work is complete and His children are ready, they will be resurrected (all of them) and receive immortal bodies, never to die or experience pain or sickness again. Because God is a successful parent, nearly all of His children will eventually be accepted back into a kingdom of glory. But not all will receive the same reward. Immortality is a free gift. Eternal life — or rather the quality of life eternal, the kind of life God lives — will depend on our faithfulness. Those who accept all God has to offer will be allowed to live with their eternal companions and will be sealed to their children and their parents in one great, eternal family (see I Corinthians 15:35 – 42, D&C 76).

What this is, in essence, is an inheritance plan, whereby our Eternal Father bequeaths to us, His children, all that he has:

> *And he that receiveth my father receiveth my father's kingdom; therefore, all that my father hath shall be given unto him.* (D&C 84:38)

So, as you load up the kids into the family van for your earthly road trip, you now have a destination in mind. Keeping your destination in sight (The Plan) and having a road map (the scriptures) by your side are two good ways to ensure everybody arrives safe and sound.

But there are warning signs: Detours ahead. Falling rock. Bridge out. Let's take a closer look at them.

Chapter 4 — Lost and Found

D ad used to tell the stories of his time in the Civilian Conservation Corps, a government work project for unemployed young men during the Depression. He and his buddies built roads, campgrounds and improvements in the Uintah mountains. They fought forest fires and planted trees. Some of the boys — my dad included — picked up a few bad habits. He was gone from home for three years, from 1934 to 1937. For much of that time, he was lost from Gospel contact. Jesus talked about Lost Sheep aka Lost Men. In fact, it was one of His most beloved parables (see Luke, chapter 15):

THEN drew near unto him all the publicans and sinners for to hear him.

And the Pharisees and scribes murmured, saying, This man receiveth sinners, and eateth with them.

And he spake this parable unto them, saying,

What man of you, having an hundred sheep, if he lose one of them, doth not leave the ninety and nine in the wilderness, and go after that which is lost, until he find it?

And when he hath found it. He layeth it on his shoulders, rejoicing.

And when he cometh home, he called together his friends and neighbours, saying unto them, Rejoice with me, for I have found my sheep which was lost.

I say unto you, that likewise joy shall be in heaven over one sinner that repenteth, more than over ninety and nine just persons, which need no repentance. (Luke 15: 1 – 7)

The sheep wasn't at fault here, not really. And neither was the shepherd. The animal just wandered off. Sometimes we all wander off — to school, to military service or to a job in a faraway city. In those situations, it is easy to get lost. If we are lucky, someone will come and find us, and we can be restored again to the flock. Sometimes, however, someone IS at fault:

Either what woman having ten pieces of silver, if she lose one piece, doth not light a candle, and sweep the house, and seek diligently till she find it?

And when she hath found it, she calleth her friends and her neighbours together, saying, Rejoice with me; for I have found the piece which I had lost.

Likewise, I say unto you, there is joy in the presence of the angels of God over one sinner that repenteth. (Luke 15:8–10)

Here we see that souls can be lost due to the neglect of others. A parent, a teacher, a Priesthood leader can fail in teaching a child or a class member correct principles. Or in a thoughtless moment, a tender person can be offended. Whatever the reason, it requires diligent effort to reclaim the lost soul.

Note one thing here: In both the case of the Lost Sheep and the Lost Coin, joy is the result when the lost item is reclaimed. I observed that joy firsthand when in 1958, my brother and my sisters were ushered into a sealing room of the Salt Lake Temple, and I saw both of my grandmothers weeping for joy as they witnessed the sealing of their grandchildren to their son and daughter.

In Jesus' last parable, a son is lost because of a conscious effort to turn away from everything a father taught him. And he has to experience the anguish of a lost soul and see firsthand the consequences of sin. It is important to remember that the father in this story has TWO sons, one who left and one faithful son who stayed behind. It is to the "good" son (evidently, the gathering of self-righteous Pharisees and scribes who scorned the savior "for receiving sinners and eating with them") to whom this parable is directed.

And he said, a certain man has two sons:

And the younger of them said to his father, Father, give me the portion of goods that falleth to me. And he divideth unto them his living.

And not many days after the younger son gathered all together, and took his journey into a far country, and there wasted his substance with riotous living.

And when he had spent all, there arose a mighty famine in that land; and he began to be in want.

And he went and joined himself to a citizen of that country; and he sent him into his fields to feed swine.

And he would have fain filled his belly with the husks that the swine did eat: and no man gave unto him.

And when he came to himself, he said, How many hired servants of my father's have bread enough and to spare, and I perish with hunger!

I will arise and go to my father, and will say unto him, Father, I have sinned against heaven and before thee,

And am no more worthy to be called they son; make me as one of thy hired servants.

And he arose, and came to his father. But when he was yet a far way off, his father saw him, and had compassion, and ran, and fell on his neck and kissed him.

And the son said unto him, Father, I have sinned against heaven, and in thy sight, and am no more worthy to be called thy son.

But the father said to his servants, Bring forth the best robe, and put it on him; and put a ring on his hand, and shoes on his feet;

And bring hither the fatted calf, and kill it; and let us eat, and be merry;

For this my son was dead, and is alive again; he was lost, and is found. And they began to be merry.

Now his elder son was in the field: and as he came and drew nigh to the house, he heard musick and dancing.

And he called one of the servants, and asked what these things meant.

And he said unto him, Thy brother is come; and thy father hath killed the fatted calf, because he he hath received him safe and sound.

And he was angry, and would not go in; therefore came his father out, and intreated him.

And he answering said unto his father, Lo, these many years do I serve thee, neither transgressed I at any times the commandments: and yet thou never gavest me a kid, that I make merry with my friends:

But as soon as this thy son was come, which hath devoured thy living with harlots, thou hast killed for him the fatted calf.

And he said unto him, Son, thou art ever with me, and all that I have is thine.

It was meet that we should make merry, and be glad: for this thy brother was dead, and is alive again; and was lost, and is found. (Luke 15:11–32)

Note the compassion of the father and the lesson he teaches "the good son." "Thy brother was dead, and is alive again; and was lost, and is found." Who cannot rejoice with a mother or father who reclaims a lost son or daughter? Truly this is joy.

There are a million ways to go wrong just as there are countless wrong answers on a math test, but only one right answer. Wide is the way and broad is the path that leadeth to destruction, the scriptures tell us. But, narrow is the way and straight is the path that leadeth to eternal life, and few there be that find it.

Does that mean that the Gospel is not for every-body, that it is some kind of an exclusive club for a handful of privileged souls? No, but it does explain one important concept: You can do it the Lord's way, or like the Prodigal Son, you can do it the hard way and spend time slopping hogs.

The Lord doesn't mince words:

And surely every man must repent or suffer, for I, God, am endless.

Wherefore, I revoke not the judgments which I shall pass, but woes shall go forth, weeping, wailing and gnashing of teeth, yea, to those who are found on my left hand. (D&C 19: 4–5)

The Prodigal Son suffered for what he did and then sought relief by returning to his father. Christ is telling us that there is a Law of Justice, which is, that every sin must be paid for, every debt paid, every transgression requited. However, some burdens are too heavy for us to bear; some sins too terrible to undo; some debts too high to repay. In other words, we are unable to satisfy the Law of Justice all by ourselves. That's why God, knowing the future and what would befall his children, prepared a Savior "from the foundation of the world."

Elder Boyd K. Packer explains it best in his wonderful parable called "The Mediator." In his story, a man borrows a great sum of money and puts off worrying about repayment. But when the debt comes due, the creditor comes calling, and he is unable to pay. He pleads for mercy, but mercy in this case only benefits him, the creditor points out. The creditor demands justice — the repayment of the debt — while the debtor pleads for mercy. Then, a third party steps forward, a beloved friend of the debtor from whom the creditor accepts the payment of the debt in full. Then, the friend offers new terms to the debtor ... terms he is able to meet.

This is the Law of Mercy, and it is available to all of us upon conditions of faith, repentance, baptism and the Holy Ghost, loving God with all our hearts and loving our fellow man as ourselves and then enduring to the end. These seven conditions are sometimes called the Laws of Adoption by which we are adopted by Christ and offered His mercy — if we do our part. The consequences of rejecting this generous offer are described in additional verses of Section 19:

> *Therefore, I command you to repent — repent, lest I smite you by the rod of my mouth, and by my wrath, and by my anger, and your sufferings be sore — how sore you know not, how exquisite you know not, yea, how hard to bear you know not.*

> *For behold, I God, have suffered these things for all, that they might not suffer if they would repent;*

> *Which suffering caused myself, even God, the greatest of all, to tremble because of pain, and to bleed at every pore, and to suffer both body and spirit — and would that I might not drink the bitter cup, and shrink —*

Nevertheless, glory be to the Father, and I partook and finished my preparations unto the children of men.

Wherefore, I command you again to repent, lest I humble you with my almighty power, and that you confess your sins, lest you suffer these punishments of which I have spoken, of which in the smallest, yea, even in the least degree you have tasted at the time I withdrew my spirit. (D&C 19:15–19)

Pay close attention to verse 16: Jesus Christ ALREADY suffered for our sins so we don't have to, upon the condition that we repent. In other words, either Jesus pays, or we pay. In any case, the bill WILL be paid. The punishment for sin is the loss of the Spirit, what Paul called "godly sorrow"... the sorrow suffered by a good person who realizes that, because of his actions, some act or word, caused an offense that led to the withdrawal of the Lord's Spirit. Call it guilt or remorse or whatever you want, but it's something most people understand.

On the other hand, as we are obedient and repentant, the Lord illuminates us with more light and spirit, "line upon line, precept upon precept" and gives us the joy God has promised His children. Repent or suffer. Joy or sorrow. Light or darkness.

The choice is ours.

Chapter 5 — Light & Darkness

The songwriter asks, "Oh say, what is truth?" When questioned by the Roman procurator Pontius Pilate who he was and why he was there, the Master said: "I am come to testify of the truth." In reply, the bewildered Roman asked, "What is truth?"

What indeed is truth? The Lord told the Prophet Joseph Smith that *"truth is knowledge of things as they are, and as they were, and as they are to come."* (D&C 93:24). We are enlightened further in the 84th-section of the Doctrine and Covenants:

> *For the word of the Lord is truth, and whatsoever is truth is light, and whatsoever is light is Spirit, even the Spirit of Jesus Christ. And the Spirit giveth light to every man that cometh into the world; and the Spirit enlighteneth every man through the world, that hearkeneth to the voice of the Spirit.* (D&C 84:45 – 46)

There are things that all men know are true on their face, things that require no explanation and no justification ... things that we know to be true thanks to the Light of Christ. We know, for example, that kindness is good and that cruelty is bad. We just know it.

There are other things that we learn from our own experience, from trial and error, truths that affect how we treat others. Moral truths.

There are scientific truths, tried and tested formulas that are true — at least for the moment — but which may be replaced with something else tomorrow. Researchers go to great length using the scientific method to eliminate error and to prove their hypotheses in an attempt to get at the truth. Through experimentation and trial and error, they try to discover truth. These are operational truths — assumptions and conclusions that are true to a 95 percent level of confidence with some possibility of error, give or take 5 percent. We use them as long as they are useful or until they are replaced by "newer" — and more accurate — truths.

Finally, there are revealed truths, specific knowledge given to man from a higher source. Sometimes they come as "the dew from heaven distilling," or as a still, small, even inaudible voice. Often, they come in a flash as an instant understanding of a concept inarticulated. On rare occasions, truth comes as a booming voice from heaven or in a vision brighter than the noonday sun.

Why does the truth come to some sooner than others? Examine again what the Lord explained in the 84th section of the Doctrine and Covenants. Verse 46 says that "the Spirit enlighteneth every man through the world, that hearkeneth to the voice of the Spirit." Revealed truth dawns upon us when we are obedient. Joseph Smith learned of the true nature of God and which church was true (he was told none of them were) because he was obedient to the admonition from the Apostle James who promised that if we want to know the truth, we should ask of God, "who giveth to all men liberally and upbraideth not, and it shall be given him" (James 1:5). Joseph held him to his word and wasn't disappointed.

Even Christ acquired truth while as a mortal upon the Earth as a result of His obedience:

And I John bear record that I beheld his glory, as the glory of the only begotten of the Father, full of grace and truth, even the Spirit of truth, which came and dwelt in the flesh, and dwelt among us.

And I, John, saw that he received not of the fullness at the first, but received grace for grace.

And he received not of the fullness at first, be continued from grace to grace, until he received a fullness.

And thus he was called the Son of God, because he received not of the fullness at the first (D&C 93:11–14)

We learn truth line upon line, precept upon precept, the scriptures tell us, a little here and a little there. As we are obedient, God confirms to us that our actions are correct, and we are blessed with greater understanding. We call this testimony. It is easier to see it in others than in ourselves.

I saw the Gospel light grow little by little in a young woman years ago in Germany. She was investigating the Gospel at the urging of her fiancé, a member of the church, but to the dismay of her parents. She was reticent about baptism — afraid might be a better word. In order to get the missionary lessons, she would ride her bike through a forest adjacent to the meetinghouse. When we were finished it was usually dark, and she would ride home through the forest by the light of her bike's generator. When we had completed our lessons, she was at first too afraid "to take the plunge" into the waters of baptism. And then a thought came to me: Every night she would jump on her bike to pedal home. It was nearly pitch black at first, but once she started pedaling, her little generator would begin to illuminate her path. As she shifted gears and picked up speed, the light would grow brighter until eventually a long cone of light led her home. I suggested to her that

that was exactly the process of living by the light. First, we have to have enough faith to start pedaling, then as we are obedient, we pick up speed until the path before us is bright and clear. But first we have to jump on the bike and start pedaling, even though initially we may find ourselves in the dark.

Jesus explained this process in Matthew 20:

... my doctrine is not mine, but his that sent me.

If any man will do his will, he shall know of the doctrine, whether it be of God, or whether I speak of myself. (Matt. 20:16–17)

In other words, faith is essential to learning and recognizing truth. It is the essential first step. As Alma said, we first have to have the desire to believe "and exercise a particle of faith... even if you can no more than desire to believe, let this desire work in you" (see Alma 32: 26–43). If we nurture the seed and let it sprout, we will soon recognize that it is a good seed, Alma teaches. Again, faith starts small and then grows.

Elder Neal A. Maxwell once said that, "God does not send thunder when a still small voice is enough." It is a careful balance, this parceling out of truth. God wants us to have just enough that we can act upon it so that He can give us more. But, He won't dump it on us.

As a character in a movie once said, "The truth?

You can't handle the truth!" God reveals truth to us line upon line, precept upon precept. As Nephi said:

> *For behold, thus saith the Lord God: I will give unto the children of men line upon line, precept upon precept, here a little and there a little; and blessed are those who hearken unto my precepts, and lend an ear unto my counsel, for they shall learn wisdom; for unto him that receiveth I will give more; and from them that shall say, We have enough, from them shall be taken away even that which they have."*
> (2 Nephi 28:30)

Obedience, in other words, brings more light; disobedience brings more darkness. God gives more light and knowledge as a blessing to the obedient "unto the perfect day." Conversely, sin chases away the Spirit, and when we sin, our minds are darkened. The apostle Paul called this "godly sorrow" or when a normally righteous person recognizes that, because of an error, he has experienced a loss of the Spirit and has seen his "spiritual lamp" grow dimmer. As the 93rd Section of the Doctrine and Covenants explains ... (verse 39) *"And that wicked one cometh and taketh away light and truth, through disobedience, from the children of men, and because of the tradition of their fathers."*

In this world of light and darkness, of truth and falsehood, good people are better able to perceive light and notice the contrast like a beam of light streaming in through a dark storm cloud. That's one of the reasons we came to this world — to learn to distinguish from the various shades of gray. Through our experience — both as a result of disobedience as well as obedience — we come to know and appreciate truth and light and learn to avoid the dark side of life:

And that which doth not edify is not of god, and is darkness.

That which is of God is light; and he that receiveth light, and continueth in God, receiveth more light; and the light groweth brighter and brighter until the perfect day.

And again, verily I say unto you, and I say it that you may know the truth, that you may chase darkness from you." (D&C 50:23-25)

The British author and moralist C.S. Lewis observed that those who are seeking the light — and act accordingly — see things more clearly than those who don't:

When a man is getting better, he understands more and more clearly the evil that is still in him. When a man is getting worse, he understands his own badness less and less. A moderately bad man knows he is not very good; a thoroughly bad man thinks he is all right. This is common sense, really. You understand sleep when you are awake, not while you are sleeping. You can see mistakes in arithmetic when your mind is working properly. While you are making them, you cannot see them, You can understand the nature of drunkenness when you are sober, not when you are drunk. Good people know about both good and evil; Bad people know about neither. (C.S. Lewis, *Mere Christianity* pg.93).

Some Christian philosophers who misunderstand the creative process and assume God that created everything out of nothing worry that if God is perfect why would His creations be imperfect, in other words, why would there be sin and darkness at all? Latter-day Saints learn from modern revelation a couple of important concepts: One, God takes "matter unorganized" and uses it in His creative process; and two, intelligence is eternal:

Man was also in the beginning with God. Intelligence , or the light of truth , was not created or made, neither indeed can be.

All truth is independent in that sphere in which God has placed it, to act for itself, as all intelligence also; otherwise there is no existence.

Behold, here is the agency of man, and here is the condemnation of man; because that which was from the beginning is plainly manifest unto them, and they receive not the light." (D&C 93:29 – 31)

LDS author and early 20th-century church leader B.H. Roberts explains that:

Evil may not be referred to God for its origin. He is not its creator; it is one of those independent existences that is uncreate and stands in the category of qualities of eternal things ... evil exists in the balance of natural forces… It is also the background of good, the incentive to good, and the trial of good, without which good could not be. ... No virtue could exist without its corresponding evil. ... In a world without evil — if such a world be really conceivable — all men would have perfect health, perfect intelligence and perfect morals. No one could gain or impart information, each one's cup of knowledge being full. The temperature would forever stand at 70 degrees, both heat and cold being evil. A world without evil would be as toil without exertion, as light without darkness, as a battle with no antagonist. It would be a world without meaning." (B.H. Roberts, *New Witnesses for God* Vol. III, p.223)

Brigham Young also taught this doctrine of opposites, or antinomy, and the importance of overcoming evil by seeking out the light. He said:

The reason of our being made subject to sin and misery, pain, woe and death, is, that we may become acquainted with the opposites of happiness and pleasure. The absence of light brings darkness, and darkness an appreciation of light; an appreciation of ease and comfort; and ignorance, falsehood, folly, and sin, in comparison with wisdom, knowledge, righteousness, and truth, make the latter the more desireable to mankind. Facts are made apparent to the human mind by their opposites." (Brigham Young, *Journal of Discourses*, Vol. 11, *p. 49*)

By understanding that God did not create evil, we can defend against attacks from jaded cynics who like to taunt believers by saying "either God is vicious because He does not want to prevent evil, or He is weak because He cannot." Free will is an eternal quality; our job — our test — is to make the right choices, to choose light instead of darkness, truth instead of falsehood, virtue instead of vice. As Hugh Nibley explains, quoting an ancient manuscript,

[God did know] that those He created would do evil… but as one who knew there was no other way to achieve the purpose for which they were created, He went ahead. He did not draw back or hesitate, nor was He afraid of what would happen. Evil is forced on no one… it is only there for those who want it. No one comes under its sway save he of his own free will deliberately subjects himself to it. (Hugh Nibley, *Collected Works of Hugh Nibley*, Vol. 2,

Ch. 21, pp 183 – 184)

We ARE free to choose — God forces no man, as the songwriter puts it:

Know this, that every soul is free
To choose his life and what he'll be;
For this eternal truth is given,
That God will force no man to heaven.
He'll call, persuade, direct aright —
Bless with wisdom, love and light
—In nameless ways be good and kind,
but never force the human mind.

— Win. C. Gregg

(Hymns, The Church of Jesus Christ of Latter-day Saints, 1979, pg. 90)

On life's path, everybody stumbles and falls occasionally. In fact, Satan takes great pleasure when we do; that's why he places obstacles along the way. We need to remember, as Elder John Widstoe explains, that:

Sin is untruth, and the misuse of truth. It decries freedom and fosters tyranny. It deceives and lies. It destroys, but never builds up except for more destruction. It slinks away from light and lurks in darkness. It is in deliberate opposition to the Lord's plan for human progress. Sin is the mark of Satan."
(John A. Widstoe, *Evidences and Reconciliations,* pg. 220)

Jesus declares in the Gospel of John that "Ye shall know the truth, and the truth shall make you free" (John 8:32). From what does the truth free us? From darkness, from ignorance, from sin. As President Joseph F. Smith said nearly a century ago:

If you love the truth, if you have received the Gospel in your hearts and love it, your intelligence will be added upon, your understanding of truth will be expanded, become larger than in any other way. Truth is the thing, above all other things in the world that makes men free. (Pres. Joseph F. Smith, *Improvement Era*, Vol. 21, pg. 102, December, 1917).

Why do some resist the light and fight against it? Why have prophets of old — and those in more recent times, Joseph Smith in particular — met with such vehement resistance? Erastus Snow, an apostle and church leader of the 19th-century said:

When the light comes to the righteous, they will hail it gladly, and though it may at first be in the distance, they will mark it as they would the dawn of the morning star, or a light shining in a dark place... while on the other hand, those who love darkness rather than light, because their deeds are evil, are fighting against the light and will shun it when it approaches, like the thief at the approach of the officer of the law, and conceals himself in darkness." (Erastus

Snow, *Journal of Discourses*, Vol. 20, April 6, 1879 *pg. 182 – 187)*

The question then is, how can we recognize light from darkness? How can we test the claims of those — Joseph Smith and his successors — who say they've found it? What is the true test of a prophet? Let's take a closer look.

Chapter 6 — The Proof of a Prophet

Forty-three years ago, I had a seminary teacher who had been a Protestant minister. He gave up everything — I mean everything — to join the Church. His name was John Heidenreich. He had had a comfortable life serving the members of his congregation in upstate New York. His ministry supplied him with a nice home, a secure job and the promise of a good retirement. Then one day, his teenage son met the Mormon missionaries, listened to what they had to say and brought home questions for his dad to answer. That changed everything. With a sincere heart, Rev. Heidenreich read the Book of Mormon and took Moroni's challenge to ask if what he had read were true. Even though it was 1963 when I last sat in his New Testament class at the Skyline High School seminary, I'll never forget his testimony:

"I asked the Lord and I got an answer," Brother Heidenreich said. "You can stay here in this beautiful garden, I was told, and help your neighbor, or you can come with me and play for higher stakes."

The Rev. Heidenreich was surprised that the Lord would use a gambling metaphor to make His point. Nevertheless, when the Lord speaks, good men listen and obey. John Heidenreich knew that taking a leap of faith was risky business. Nobody (but the Lord) knows what the future might hold. But, Rev. Heidenreich knew what it meant for him: It meant giving up his livelihood, his home, his retirement — everything.

But he did it anyway.

He resigned his ministry, packed up everything he could into the family station wagon and headed west. Somewhere in Ohio, the car's engine blew. Finally, after it was fixed, the unemployed ex-minister arrived in Salt Lake City and found a place to live: a dingy motel room. They stayed there a year until the Church Education System made an exception for him. Because of his training and education, he was hired as an LDS seminary teacher. A year or two later, he arrived at Skyline High School.

John Heidenreich was willing to bet on the Lord; he took a giant leap of faith.

Change is always risky business. In my own family, my father at the age of 41 responded to the kind promptings of members of the Rosecrest 2nd Ward in the Canyon Rim area. A good bishop, a diligent Senior Aaronic Priesthood leader and loving hometeachers all helped him make the leap of faith to activity. Throughout the scriptures, we read where the Lord challenges His people to take a risk, to experiment upon His words. There is always a reward attached to that challenge.

Alma invited a group of poor Nephites ... "to try an experiment" on the Lord's word — to put Him to the test.

Now, as I said concerning faith — that it was not a perfect knowledge — even so it is with my words. Ye cannot know of their surety at first, unto perfection, any more than faith is a perfect knowledge.

But behold, if ye will awake and arouse your faculties, even to an experiment upon my words, and exercise a particle of faith, yea, even if ye can no more than desire to believe, let this desire work in you, even until ye believe in a manner that ye can give place for a portion of my words.

Now, we will compare the word unto a seed. Now, if ye give place, that a seed may be planted in your heart, behold, if it be a true seed, or a good seed, if ye do not cast it out by your unbelief, that ye will resist the Spirit of the Lord, behold, it will begin to swell within your breasts; and when you feel these swelling motions, ye will begin to say within yourselves—It must needs be that this is a good seed, or that the word is good, for it beginneth to enlarge my soul; yea, it beginneth to enlighten my understanding, yea, it beginneth to be delicious to me. (Alma 32: 26 – 29)

Note that word: "experiment."

The process of trial and error is key to the scientific method. Generally, a researcher will begin an experiment or test after observing something in nature. Then he or she will develop a hypothesis, followed by a testing procedure. A statistical model will then be set up ahead of time to measure the results; if they fall within a narrow range of acceptable risk, then the experiment has proven its point, or hypothesis.

What is the hypothesis before us, then? In question form, it is: Was Joseph Smith what he said he was, a prophet, seer and revelator who translated an ancient book of scripture, the Book of Mormon, and received power from on high to re-establish God's kingdom on Earth? Consider what's at stake, look at the promises inherent with this Good News (that's the meaning of the Gospel — the Good News). No other religious body in the world promises as much and describes the rewards in such detail: These promises include life eternal sealed to a spouse and children and clothed in a glorified resurrected body, generations linked together, worlds of glory, all that the Father has bequeathed to His worthy children. It is an optimistic, cheery look at eternity. Isn't that worth checking out? Too many people dismiss it out of hand with a shrug and a wave with the comment, "God doesn't talk to anybody anymore — and if He did, why would He pick an ignorant American farmboy? It's just too good to be true!"

What if a stranger knocked on your door and told you a long-lost relative — an uncle or a great-grandfather — left you a fortune of millions of dollars and acres of rolling farmland, would you shut the door in his face? Or would you check out his story?

In my father's case, he was in the hospital after having undergone major surgery due to a perforated ulcer. He had made the commitment to "get active" and take his family to the temple. But, he still had questions. He wondered why the Lord had not left the golden plates from which the Book of Mormon had been translated on the Earth so people could see and touch them and know for a certainty what Joseph had claimed was true. Then, he said, the answer came directly and clearly: One, if the plates had been left, we would have people disputing the translation and clamoring for "experts" to do their own translation — with multiple translations around (not to mention thieves attempting to nab the priceless objects); and two, there are very few (if any) **original** manuscripts from the Bible around to prove its authenticity. The proof of both books comes from their contents, not some original manuscript (which only experts — if they existed — could verify) or some external evidence. In other words, you have to put the contents to a test of faith by reading and applying the principles found therein in order to validate them.

That's why Joseph Smith described the Book of Mormon as the keystone of our religion. A keystone is the wedge-shaped rock at the top of an arch that holds the whole structure together. Take it out, the arch falls apart. However, if you can prove its truth, the whole structure is validated.

That takes us to the point of this discussion: **What is the proof of a prophet?** How can an ordinary person validate the claims made by Joseph Smith?

Let's start with the hypothesis described above, namely, that Joseph Smith was indeed a prophet and his testimony is true, and therefore so is the church he founded. In a testing situation, researchers generally set up a null hypothesis — the opposite of the hypothesis — and run their experiments to disprove it. In this case, the null hypothesis is: Joseph Smith was NOT a prophet. Logic demands that if you can disprove the null hypothesis to a certain degree of statistical certainty, then **you must accept the test hypothesis**, in this case that Joseph Smith WAS INDEED A PROPHET OF GOD, just as he claimed. If you can't disprove the null hypothesis with limited facts, you can look for more data, set it aside for now or accept it. But, in any case, you allow for error. The key is understanding what's at stake, and what the consequences of your errors are. In statistics, researchers describe two kinds of error: A **Type I** error, which is **rejecting the null hypothesis** (and accepting the test hypothesis) **when you should have accepted it**; and, a **Type II** error, **accepting the null hypothesis when you should have rejected it**. The amount of time, money and effort in the testing process is measured against the consequences of making the wrong decision. When the test is finished, the researchers will state that they are 95 percent certain of their conclusion. But, there's always a 5 percent chance your methods were wrong, you had a bad sample or you ran the wrong test.

The point is, you must know beforehand what the consequences are of making an error — either Type I or Type II. Note the chart comparing Type I and Type II errors on the next page:

COMPARISON OF TYPE I & TYPE II ERRORS

CORRECT DECISION VS. WRONG DECISION	
NULL HYPOTHESIS **J. Smith WAS NOT** **a Prophet** **ACCEPT IF FALSE** **NO ERROR**	**TEST HYPOTHESIS:** **J. Smith WAS** **a Prophet** **ACCEPT IF TRUE** **NO ERROR**
NULL HYPOTHESIS: **J. Smith WAS NOT** **a Prophet** **REJECT IF TRUE** **TYPE I ERROR**	**TEST HYPOTHESIS:** **J. Smith WAS** **a Prophet** **ACCEPT IF FALSE** **TYPE II ERROR**

What does this mean to people seeking the truth?

Type I error: Rejecting the null hypothesis — that Joseph Smith WAS NOT a prophet — and therefore **accepting in error his claims and embracing the church when it is not what it says it is.** What are the costs of this theoretical incorrect decision? Ten percent of your income, time wasted in church and in service, unnecessary family home evenings held, missed earthly pleasures you decided to forego because of a false promise of an eternal reward, and perhaps not following some other course of religious action (Catholicism, Protestantism, Judaism, Islam etc. or none at all).

Type II error: Now weigh those costs against the **Type II error of accepting the null hypothesis and rejecting the prophet Joseph Smith and the blessings of the true church when in fact, it is all true just as Joseph and millions of Saints have testified.** What would you give up? First, the peace of mind and contentment most faithful Latter-day Saints say they enjoy through obedience to the laws and ordinances of the Gospel; second, an improved family life and organization that people generally experience in LDS families as well as the improved physical and mental health derived from living the Word of Wisdom and the Law of Chastity as taught by the church; and last, the blessings of eternal family life and the promised inheritance from your Heavenly Father of all that He has! (see D&C 84:39). Those are risks worth weighing, aren't they?

To help you choose wisely, please examine the following exhibits or evidence. Remember, the purpose here is to test the null hypothesis, so ask yourself this question: **What are the odds that a false prophet could have accomplished all this?** Christ said "by their fruits ye shall know them." So examine these fruits carefully! Weigh this evidence. A lot hangs in the balance. It is my belief that as you do so honestly with a humble heart, you will reject the null hypothesis and therefore accept Joseph's testimony and the message of the Restoration along with all its associated blessings.

Exhibit No. 1 — The Book of Mormon: The 400+ pages of this book illuminate doctrine lost, forgotten or misunderstood by the sectarian world, such things as an explanation of the resurrection, the nature and mission of Jesus Christ, the relationship between mercy and justice (mercy cannot rob justice), reason for pain and suffering, the need for a second witness and the need for continuous revelation (line upon line, precept upon precept). The content of the book alone is witness to its truthfulness. B.H. Roberts pointed to just a few kernels of wisdom in the Book of Mormon that rival anything in the Bible or literature. These "aphorisms" are priceless gems. Read them for yourself and ask this question: Could a false prophet manufacture something this profound?

- *Adam fell that men might be; and men are, that they might have joy* (2 Nephi 2:25).

- *It must needs be, that there is an opposition in all things* (2 Nephi 2:11).

- *When you are in the service of your fellow beings you are only in the service of your God* (Mosiah 2:17).

- *Wickedness never was happiness* (Alma 41:10).

- *To be learned is good if they hearken unto the counsels of God* (2 Nephi 9:29).

- *It is by grace that we are saved, after all we can do.* (2 Nephi 25:23).

- *See that ye bridle all your passions, that ye may be filled with love* (Alma 38:12).

- *What manner of men ought ye to be? Verily I say unto you, even as I am* (3 Nephi 27:27).

- *I give unto men weaknesses that they may be humble; . . . for if they humble themselves before me, and have faith in me, then will I make weak things become strong unto them* (Ether 12:27).

- *Despair cometh because of iniquity.* (Moroni 10:22)

- *Without faith there cannot be any hope.* (Moroni 7:42).

- *Charity is the pure love of Christ, and it endureth forever; and whoso is found possessed of it at the last day, it shall be well with him.* (Moroni 7:47)

- *The laborer in Zion shall labor for Zion; for if they labor for money they shall perish.* (2 Nephi 26:31)

Exhibit No. 2: The Doctrine & Covenants and the Pearl of Great Price — Two more books of scripture lay out doctrine and explain concepts which the sectarian world has stumbled over for more than 1500 years, such as the nature of the Godhead, the eternal nature of man, the glories God has in store for His faithful children; a just plan for the distribution of goods to care for the poor, an explanation of intelligence, light and glory that are at the core of who we are. Where did all this come from if not from God? Certainly not from an uneducated farm boy! Again, reading is the proof of the pudding.

Exhibit No. 3: Joseph's prophetic utterances — Most people think of a prophet as a predictor of future events, when actually the meaning is much broader and deeper than that. Nevertheless, Joseph's prophetic utterances deserve closer inspection and demonstrate his prophetic gift of foreseeing future events, such as these:

- The Book of Mormon would be published worldwide and that this record "would go to every nation, and kindred, and tongue and people under the heaven," according to what Joseph said the Angel Moroni prophesied at their very first meeting.

- Joseph's name would be had for good or evil throughout the world, that "the workers of iniquity will seek your overthrow... seek to destroy your reputation...will seek your life." These words, Joseph said, were uttered by Moroni to him at their first meeting in September, 1823 and first published in 1834, long before they were proved true.

- The church would grow into a worldwide organization (See Exhibit No. 5); its success is itself a fulfillment of prophecy. As Moroni prophesied to Joseph, the church will "spread farther and farther" despite opposition and persecution.

- "A great and marvelous work is about to come forth." This statement precedes several sections of the Doctrine and Covenants, given at the very beginning of church history. Even enemies of the church would have to concede that it is, in fact, great and marvelous.

- Wars, rumors of wars, and in particular, the American Civil War were predicted by the prophet. On Christmas Day in 1832, after Joseph made inquiries of the Lord on trouble in the land, he said he received the following revelation:

VERILY, thus saith the Lord concerning the wars that will shortly come to pass, beginning at the rebellion of South Carolina, which will eventually terminate in the death and misery of many souls;

And the time will come that war will be poured out upon all nations, beginning at this place.

For behold the Southern States shall be divided against the Northern States, and the Southern States will call upon other nations, even the nation of Great Britain, as it is called, and they shall also call upon other nations in order to defend themselves against other nations, and then shall war be poured out upon all nations. (D&C 87: 1 – 3)

- Another verse given earlier corroborates the same thing: *Ye hear of wars in foreign lands; but, behold, I say unto you, they are nigh, even at your doors, and not many years hence ye shall hear of wars in your own lands.* (D&C 45:63)

- Finally, note what Joseph records in the first section of the Doctrine and Covenants of the prophecies he says he has received:

Search these commandments, for they are true and faithful, and the prophecies and promises which are in them shall all be fulfilled.

What I the Lord have spoken, I have spoken, and I excuse not myself; and though the heavens and the earth pass away, my word shall not pass away, but shall all be fulfilled, whether by mine own voice or by the voice of my servants, it is the same. (D&C 1: 37 – 38)

Exhibit No. 4: The Word of Wisdom — Who knew in 1833 about nicotine or caffeine? Who could have predicted the conspiracy of the tobacco industry to enslave billions of people that corporate whistle-blowers have uncovered? And yet that was prophesied in the 89th-section of the Doctrine and Covenants by a young man without any medical training through the gift and power of God. Statistics bear out how the Word of Wisdom — the call for Latter-day Saints to abstain from alcohol, tobacco, coffee and tea and to eat healthy grains, fruits and vegetables — was indeed wise advice. Utahns continue to be the healthiest of people with lower incidences of heart disease, lung cancer and other ailments caused or exacerbated by the substances banned by the Word of Wisdom. Was that just a lucky call by "a false prophet," or was it divine providence?

Exhibit No. 5: Church growth — In 1984, University of Washington sociologist Rodney Stark noted that "today there are more than 5 million

Mormons on Earth. How many will there be in the near future? Projections require assumptions. If growth during the next century is like the past, the Mormons will become a major world faith. If, for example, we assume they will grow by 30 percent per decade, then in 2080, there will be more than 60 million Mormons. But, since World War II, the Mormon growth rate has been far higher than 30 percent per decade. If we set the rate at 60 percent, then in 2080, there will be 265 million Mormons." And then he adds that anyone in 1880 (when LDS membership numbered about 160,000) who had predicted that it would grow to 5 million in a century, would have been ridiculed.

Taking Stark decade-by-decade compound growth projections and updating actual numbers (36 percent), that would mean by its 200th birthday, church membership could easily reach 47 million."

A media report from the National Council of Churches observed in 2002 that the LDS church had grown to the fifth largest denomination in the United States, noting "this ranking represents a very brisk increase in membership for a church with a relatively brief history." The spokesperson attributes church growth to "the distinct theological position of the

LDS... and its emphasis on outreach (missionary work)."

Exhibit No. 6: The Church's focus on the family — No other organization anywhere has been more family-friendly than The Church of Jesus Christ of Latter-day Saints. It is just common sense, or is it providential that church leaders saw early on the effects of the assault on the family and society as a whole. Church President David O. McKay coined a phrase a generation ago that still rings true today: "No other success can compensate for failure in the home." Long before national commentators were tuned into "family values," the church was preaching and practicing family-friendly principles.

Exhibit No. 7: Biblical prophecies fulfilled — Old and New Testament prophecies predicted both the apostasy from Christ's church and its restoration. The Prophet Isaiah envisions "a marvelous work and a wonder" and saw the day when the "deaf [will] hear the works of the book, and eyes of the blind shall see out of the darkness." In that same chapter (Isaiah 29), he predicts a sealed book would be taken to a learned man (Prof. Charles Anthon) who could not read it but would be taken to an unlearned man who could (Joseph Smith). Ezekiel speaks of the "stick of Judah" (the Bible) and the "stick of Joseph" (the Book of Mormon) be combined together (like a quadruple combination!). Jesus tells of having "other sheep not of this fold; them must I also bring... and there shall be one fold and one shepherd." Latter-day Saints believe those people to be the Book of Mormon peoples. And Peter predicts in Acts that before the Savior comes again, "there must be a restitution of all things." If something weren't lost, why would it have to be restored? The Bible — when you read it carefully with the Spirit — testifies to the mission of the Prophet Joseph Smith.

Exhibit No. 8: The witnesses of the Book of Mormon — Eleven other men besides Joseph Smith testified to the truthfulness of the Book of Mormon. Eight of them saw the plates and the translators; three others saw the plates and saw the Angel Moroni who testified to the truthfulness of the work (the translation of the Book of Mormon and the role of the prophet Joseph Smith). As Oliver Cowdery, David Whitmer and Martin Harris testified, "we know that they have been translated by the gift and power of God ... we testify that we have seen the engravings ... we declare with words of soberness that an Angel of God came down from heaven. ..." Those three men either bore a true witness or they lied — there's no room for political parsing of words or misunderstanding.

You either buy it or you don't. But choose wisely: There's a lot on the line!

Exhibit No. 9: The martyrdom — On June 27th, 1844, the prophet Joseph Smith and his brother Hyrum Smith gave their lives for their testimonies, sealing their missions with their blood as ancient prophets, apostles and saints had done. A verse in the 135th-section of the Doctrine and Covenants gives them this tribute:

Joseph Smith, the Prophet and Seer of the Lord, has done more, save Jesus only, for the salvation of men in this world, than any other man that ever lived in it. In the short space of twenty years, he has brought forth the Book of Mormon, which he translated by the gift and power of God, and has been the means of publishing it on two continents; has sent the fullness of the everlasting gospel, which it contained, to the four quarters of the earth; has brought forth the revelations and commandments which compose this book of Doctrine and Covenants, and many other wise documents and instructions for the benefit of the children of men; gathered many thousands of the Latter-day Saints, founded a great city, and left a fame and name that cannot be slain. He lived great, and he died great in the eyes of God and his people; and like most of the Lord's anointed in ancient times, has sealed his mission and his works with his own blood; and so has his brother Hyrum. In life they were not divided, and in death they were not separated. (D&C 135:5)

One simple question: Would a false prophet give up his life for a lie? Think about it.

Exhibit No. 10: Moroni's and Joseph's testimonies — Joseph attributes much of what he preached and prophesied to an ancient American prophet named Moroni. If the Book of Mormon is indeed the keystone of the LDS religion, then Moroni's promise is the key to knowing if the book is what it claims to be. Moroni made this promise to all who receive his and his father's (Mormon's) record:

> *And when ye shall receive these things, I would exhort you that ye would ask God, the Eternal Father, in the name of Christ, if these things are not true; and if ye shall ask with a sincere heart, with real intent, having faith in Christ, he will manifest the truth of it unto you, by the power of the Holy Ghost.*

> *And by the power of the Holy Ghost ye may know the truth of all things. (Moroni 10: 4 – 5)*

And finally, no trial would be complete — or convincing — without the defendant testifying of his innocence. In his own words, Joseph Smith defends his claim of a divine calling as he tells of the persecution near his New York home when he told others of his First Vision:

It caused me serious reflection then, and often has since, how very strange it was that an obscure boy, of a little over fourteen years of age, and one, too, who was doomed to the necessity of obtaining a scanty maintenance by his daily labor, should be thought a character of sufficient importance to attract the attention of the great ones of the most popular sects of the day, and in a manner to create in them a spirit of the most bitter persecution and reviling . But strange or not, so it was, and it was often the cause of great sorrow to myself.

However, it was nevertheless a fact that I had beheld a vision. I have thought since, that I felt much like Paul, when he made his defense before King Agrippa, and related the account of the vision he had when he saw a light, and heard a voice; but still there were but few who believed him; some said he was dishonest, others said he was mad; and he was ridiculed and reviled. But all this did not destroy the reality of his vision. He had seen a vision, he knew he had, and all the cpersecution under heaven could not make it otherwise; and though they should persecute him unto death, yet he knew, and would know to his latest breath, that he had both seen a light and heard a voice speaking unto him, and all the world could not make him think or believe otherwise.

So it was with me. I had actually seen a light, and in the midst of that light I saw two Personages, and they did in reality speak to me; and though I was hated and persecuted for saying that I had seen a vision, yet it was true; and while they were persecuting me, reviling me, and speaking all manner of evil against me falsely for so saying, I was led to say in my heart: Why persecute me for telling the truth? I have actually seen a vision; and who am I that I can withstand God, or why does the world think to make me deny what I have actually seen? For I had seen a vision; I knew it, and I knew that God knew it, and I could not deny it, neither dared I do it; at least I knew that by so doing I would offend God, and come under condemnation.

I had now got my mind satisfied so far as the sectarian world was concerned — that it was not my duty to join with any of them, but to continue as I was until further directed. I had found the testimony of James to be true — that a man who lacked wisdom might ask of God, and obtain, and not be upbraided. (Joseph Smith History 23 – 26)

Now ask, is there sufficient evidence to reject the null hypothesis and accept the premise and claim by Joseph Smith that he was, in fact, what he said he was, a prophet called by God to translate the Book of Mormon, receive revelation and the necessary keys to bring about the restoration of Christ's church on Earth? If so, what's next?

Chapter 7 — Stumbling Blocks

Once you have determined to chart a course towards the Straight and Narrow Path, you will undoubtedly find obstacles strewn along the way. Boulders, pitfalls, stumps, maybe even a washed out gully. For many, the journey is just too hard, and they fall by the wayside. For some, they're stumbling blocks that slow them down. But others use them as stepping stones.

Why is one man's stumbling block another's stepping stone? The late Elder Neal A. Maxwell had some thoughts on the subject:

A stumbling block appears when we serve God generously with time and checkbooks but still withhold portions of our inner selves, signifying that we are not yet fully His!

He notes the necessity of our submitting to the will of the Father if we want to find our way:

Spiritual submissiveness is not accomplished in an instant, but by the incremental improvements and by the successive use of stepping-stones. Stepping-stones are meant to be taken one at a time anyway. Eventually our wills can be

*"swallowed up in the will of the Father" as we are "willing
to submit ... even as a child doth submit to his father.*
(Elder Neal A. Maxwell, Consecrate Thy
Performance, *Ensign*, May 2002, pg. 36)

Are we on the path when we hold back, when we
are only willing to go part way? The story is told of a
rich, young prince who, after listening to Jesus,
desires to know what's next for him. The story unfolds
in Matthew:

*And, behold, one came and said unto him, Good Master,
what good thing shall I do, that I may have eternal life?*

*And he said unto him, Why callest thou me good? there is
none good but one, that is, God: but if thou wilt enter into
life, keep the commandments.*

*He saith unto him, Which? Jesus said, Thou shalt do no
murder , Thou shalt not commit adultery, Thou shalt not
steal, Thou shalt not bear false witness,*

*Honour thy father and thy mother: and, Thou shalt love
thy neighbour as thyself.*

*The young man saith unto him, All these things have I
kept from my youth up: what lack I yet?*

*Jesus said unto him, If thou wilt be perfect, go and sell that
thou hast, and give to the poor, and thou shalt have treasure in heaven: and come and follow me.*

But when the young man heard that saying, he went away sorrowful: for he had great possessions. (Matt 19:16 – 22)

His possessions were a stumbling block — not stepping stones as they are for so many generous people — on the way to the straight and narrow path. How many of us have placed obstacles on our path that make us stumble and fall, such as ...?

- A lack of understanding

- A misunderstanding

- A bad habit

- A serious misdeed, an unrepented transgression

- An unkind comment, a cruel criticism that can't be forgiven

- Fear, apprehension

- An unplanned detour resulting in spiritual forgetfulness

- A love of the world, materialism

- And pride!

Pick your poison: The effect is the same if it keeps us from getting back on the path that leads us to joy and happiness. A woman once bore her testimony about her struggles in self improvement and admitted: "I'm now working on my last, few favorite sins." What are yours?

Most of the stumbling blocks that prevent so many from

enjoying full fellowship with the Saints can be filed under one of the three parables described in chapter 4: The Lost Sheep, The Lost Coin and the Prodigal Son. Sometimes we wander off; sometimes our lost state is the result of neglect by someone else: a parent, a teacher or an acquaintance who failed us in some way. But sometimes it is the result of willful transgression. How often do home teachers, parents, siblings and friends try to help us with our stumbling blocks in vain? No matter how much others want to help, we have to take the first step. The good news is we don't have to do it alone — we have help, in fact, it's all around us — maybe even closer than we think.

The Barney Clark family can attest to that. Does that name ring a bell? Dr. Clark, a dentist, made headlines around the world when he became the first recipient of an artificial heart. But, in an Ensign article in 1986, his untold story is about the softening of his heart and his return to the Gospel fold a short while before his operation.

Because he smoked, he felt unworthy to go to church, Una Loy Barney said about her husband. "So he would always have a reason not to go with us on Sunday. But, he insisted that we pay our tithing, and he supported me as I worked in the Church." In the end, Dr. Clark was befriended by a fellow dentist who "got me [him] to do things I ought to do and like it," Dr. Barney said. A combination of a loving family, friends in the ward and a life-threatening disease all helped soften his "spiritual" heart before his earthly heart eventually gave out. But before he died, his loving wife's life-long prayer was answered when she and her husband went to the temple:

"To me, it was as if we were already in heaven together," she said. "It was an emotional experience that I will never forget and one that has been a comfort to me now that he is gone." (Giles H. Florence Jr., "The Softening of the Heart," *Ensign*, July 1986, p. 12)

A softened heart — or as it is sometimes described, a broken heart and a contrite spirit — is a necessary lever to lodge pride out of the way as we trudge forward to the Straight and Narrow Path.

In Lehi's dream, "a large and spacious building" stands for the pride of the world and the vain imaginations of men where people in fine clothing laugh and point at others below them striving to grab hold of the iron rod that leads to the Tree of Life. Lehi sees other hazards, too, such as "a great mist of darkness," a "fountain of filthy waters" each representing, respectively, "the depths of hell" and the "temptations of the devil." And there are forbidden paths where souls wander off and get lost.

Lehi's concerns in his dreams are for two of his sons, Laman and Lemuel, who despite his pleadings to press forward, join others in mocking "numberless concourses of people, many of whom were pressing forward, that they might obtain the path which led unto the tree by which I stood." Lehi was anguishing over his sons:

And it came to pass after my father had spoken all the words of his dream or vision, which were many , he said unto us, because of these things which he saw in a vision, he exceedingly feared for Laman and Lemuel; yea, he feared lest they should be cast off from the presence of the Lord.

And he did exhort them then with all the feeling of a tender parent, that they would hearken to his words, that perhaps the Lord would be merciful to them, and not cast them off; yea, my father did preach unto them. (I Nephi 8:37–38)

Of all the stumbling blocks — the Word of Wisdom, moral transgressions, personal tragedy, being wronged by someone in authority — pride is the one with the deepest roots. It is like a huge oak stump that can't be pulled out with a tractor and a chain. Its roots have to be hacked away first.

Pres. Ezra Taft Benson focused on "everyone's last, favorite sin" in a brilliant conference talk in April, 1989.

When pride has a hold on our hearts, we lose our independence of the world and deliver our freedoms to the bondage of men's judgment. The world shouts louder than the whisperings of the Holy Ghost. The reasoning of men overrides the revelations of God, and the proud let go of the iron rod.

Pride is a sin that can readily be seen in others but is rarely admitted in ourselves. Most of us consider pride to be a sin of those on the top, such as the rich and the learned, looking down at the rest of us (see 2 Ne. 9:42). There is, however, a far more common ailment among us — and that is pride from the bottom looking up. It is manifest in so many ways, such as faultfinding, gossiping, backbiting, murmuring, living beyond our means, envying, coveting, withholding gratitude and praise that might lift another, and being unforgiving and jealous.

Disobedience is essentially a prideful power struggle against someone in authority over us. It can be a parent, a priesthood leader, a teacher, or ultimately God. A proud person hates the fact that someone is above him. He thinks this lowers his position.

The proud make every man their adversary by pitting their intellects, opinions, works, wealth, talents, or any other worldly measuring device against others. In the words of C. S. Lewis: Pride gets no pleasure out of having something, only out of having more of it than the next man. ... It is the comparison that makes you proud: the pleasure of being above the rest. Once the element of competition has gone, pride has gone."

Pride is the universal sin, the great vice. Yes, pride is the universal sin, the great vice.

The antidote for pride is humility—meekness, submissiveness. (see Alma 7:23) It is the broken heart and contrite spirit. (Pres. Ezra Taft Benson, "Pride", *Ensign,* April 1989)

When the former Rev. John Heidenreich, was considering baptism, he had a lingering question that was bothering him: the sacrament. In his church and as described in the New Testament, bread and wine were served in remembrance of the Savior. And, then when he attended an LDS sacrament meeting, it was bread and water. Water? Why water? He couldn't get past that. So, he took the matter to the Lord. And he got an answer. He had a dream of the Savior on the cross and saw when the Roman guard pierced the Lord's side after he died and out came water, mixed with blood. Some scholars have commented that was the result of Christ's dying of a broken heart. In modern scripture, we are asked not to sacrifice animals on the altar as did the Israelites in ancient times, but rather "to offer a broken heart and contrite spirit." Lehi explains to his son,

Jacob, in II Nephi 2 why a broken heart and a contrite spirit are so important:

Wherefore, redemption cometh in and through the Holy Messiah; for he is full of grace and truth.

Behold, he offereth himself a sacrifice for sin, to answer the ends of the law, unto all those who have a broken heart and a contrite spirit; and unto none else can the ends of the law be answered.

Wherefore, how great the importance to make these things known unto the inhabitants of the earth, that they may know that there is no flesh that can dwell in the presence of God, save it be through the merits, and mercy, and grace of the Holy Messiah, who layeth down his life according to the flesh, and taketh it again by the power of the Spirit , that he may bring to pass the resurrection of the dead, being the first that should rise.

Wherefore, he is the firstfruits unto God, inasmuch as he shall make intercession for all the children of men; and they that believe in him shall be saved. (2 Nephi 2:6 – 9)

Rev. Heidenreich learned then what the Lord required of him. What does he require of you? Read the words of Nephi who was taught by Christ what is required of all of us:

But, behold, my beloved brethren, thus came the voice of the

Son unto me, saying: After ye have repented of your sins, and witnessed unto the Father that ye are willing to keep my commandments, by the baptism of water, and have received the baptism of fire and of the Holy Ghost, and can speak with a new tongue, yea, even with the tongue of angels, and after this should deny me, it would have been better for you that ye had not known me.

And I heard a voice from the Father, saying: Yea, the words of my Beloved are true and faithful. He that endureth to the end, the same shall be saved.

And now, my beloved brethren, I know by this that unless a man shall endure to the end, in following the example of the Son of the living God, he cannot be saved.

Wherefore, do the things which I have told you I have seen that your Lord and your Redeemer should do; for this cause have they been shown unto me, that ye might know the gate by which ye should enter. For the gate by which ye should enter is repentance and baptism by water; and then cometh a remission of your sins by fire and by the Holy Ghost.

And then are ye in this strait and narrow path which leads to eternal life; yea, ye have entered in by the gate; ye have done according to the commandments of the Father and the Son; and ye have received the Holy Ghost, which witnesses of the Father and the Son, unto the fulfilling of the promise which he hath made, that if ye entered in by the way ye should receive.

And now, my beloved brethren, after ye have gotten into this strait and narrow path, I would ask if all is done? Behold, I say unto you, Nay; for ye have not come thus far save it were by the word of Christ with unshaken faith in him, relying wholly upon the merits of him who is mighty to save.

Wherefore, ye must press forward with a steadfastness in Christ, having a perfect brightness of hope, and a love of God and of all men. Wherefore, if ye shall press forward, feasting upon the word of Christ, and endure to the end, behold, thus saith the Father: Ye shall have eternal life. (2 Nephi 31:14 – 20)

Press forward. Endure to the end. A broken heart and a contrite spirit. That's a prescription for making changes in our lives. Change is hard, especially when we are set in our ways and comfortable with our imperfections. But, it is possible.

And, it is essential. The good news about making a major course correction in life is that we do not have to do it alone. We have help. Family, friends, ward members, Priesthood leaders, and most important, our Savior Jesus Christ.

He taught us the way, the truth and the life. If we want to change, we have to follow Him.

Chapter 8 — A Changed Man

He came by night, this leader of the Jews, to ask Jesus questions he dared not raise in the light of day. His conversation with the Savior is one of the most famous passages in holy writ.

His name was Nicodemus, described by John as a man of the Pharisees ... a ruler of the Jews:

The same came to Jesus by night, and said unto him, Rabbi, we know that thou art a teacher come from God: for no man can do these miracles that thou doest, except God be with him.

Jesus answered and said unto him, Verily, verily, I say unto thee, Except a man be born again, he cannot see the kingdom of God.

Nicodemus saith unto him, How can a man be born when he is old? Can he enter the second time into his mother's womb, and be born?

Jesus answered, Verily, verily, I say unto thee, Except a man be born of water and of the Spirit , he cannot enter into the kingdom of God. (John 3:2 – 5)

Despite his age, his standing and his wealth, Nicodemus held out hope that even for him, there was the possibility of change. "How can a man be born again when he is old?" How indeed? Does life offer us Mulligans, a chance to take that first T-shot over again and not have to take a stroke? That question — can a man be born again — has been posed by Christians for centuries.

I watched my own father, at the age of 41, take the necessary, painful steps to change. He had been sickly his whole life; he suffered from ulcers, a condition that led to his honorable discharge from the army during World War II. He was in Officers Candidate School and wanted to join the fight in Europe.

But it wasn't to be.

In 1957, he was challenged to become worthy to ordain me a deacon, and the effort to quit smoking exacerbated his ulcers, sent him to the hospital and resulted in surgery. In recovery, he found he couldn't stand the smell of tobacco smoke and never touched the foul weed again. Change can be painful. Later, I watched as he learned to walk again after a stroke. He was able to change his course in life because the pain of remaining the way he was was greater than taking a new direction.

Change is about taking responsibility for our own situation in life. The second Article of Faith spells it out plainly: "We believe that men will be punished for their own sins and not for Adam's transgression." Elder Dean L. Larsen, formerly of the Seventy, noted that...

> *When we understand what is right and what is wrong, we are in a position to exercise our freedom in making choices. In so doing, we must stand accountable for our decisions, and we cannot escape the inevitable consequences of these choices. Such freedom to exercise moral agency is essential in an environment where people have the highest prospects for progress and development.* (Elder Dean L. Larsen, *Ensign*, May 1980, pg. 76.)

Christ showed us the way by making correct choices — he wasn't forced or compelled to be obedient. Like us, He had his free agency. President Howard W. Hunter explains:

> *It is important to remember that Jesus was capable of sinning, that he could have succumbed, that the plan of life and salvation could have been foiled, but that he remained true. Had there been no possibility of his yielding to the enticement of Satan, there would have been no real test, no genuine victory in the result. If he had been stripped of the faculty to sin, he would have been stripped of his very*

agency. It was he who had come to safeguard and ensure the agency of man. He had to retain the capacity and ability to sin had he willed so to do.

As Paul wrote, Though he were a Son, yet learned he obedience by the things which he suffered (Heb. 5:8); and he was in all points tempted like as we are, yet without sin (Heb. 4:15). He was perfect and sinless, not because he had to be, but rather because he clearly and determinedly wanted to be. The Doctrine and Covenants records, He suffered temptations but gave no heed unto them. (D&C 20:22.) (Pres. Howard W. Hunter, "The Temptations of Christ," *Ensign,* Nov. 1976, pg. 17)

For every person who ever lived, change begins from within, as President Ezra Taft Benson observes:

The Lord works from the inside out. The world works from the outside in. The world would take people out of the slums. Christ takes the slums out of people, and then they take themselves out of the slums. The world would mold men by changing their environment. Christ changes men, who then change their environment. The world would shape human behavior, but Christ can change human nature. (Ezra Taft Benson,"Born of God," *Tambuli,* Oct. 1989, pg. 2)

It is easy to blame our mistakes on our fallen nature, on a sad childhood, on a Sunday School teacher that scolded us, on peers in our youth that rejected us. But it doesn't hold water. As King Benjamin explains in Mosiah in the Book of Mormon:

> *For the natural man is an enemy to God, and has been from the fall of Adam, and will be, forever and ever, unless he yields to the enticings of the Holy Spirit, and putteth off the natural man and becometh a saint through the atonement of Christ the Lord, and becometh as a child, submissive, meek, humble, patient, full of love, willing to submit to all things which the Lord seeth fit to inflict upon him, even as a child doth submit to his father.* (Mosiah 3:19)

I believe this means that we have the responsibility to change; but, it also explains that there is help — we don't have to go it alone! We have to yield to the enticings of the Holy Spirit. This is the first inkling of hope that we have — the light at the end of the proverbial tunnel.

As a person who is an expert dieter — I have started many diets over and over again, some even with a small measure of success, usually followed by a weight gain — I am intrigued by pictures of success, of before-and-after pictures of people who have lost 30, 40, 50 pounds or more. I say to myself, I want to be like that (the AFTER pictures)! We all wish for a magic pill, but deep inside we know that for most of us, it means exercise and eating less. But this isn't a diet book!

This is a book about taking Christ at his word and putting off the old man and taking on the new. The Prophet Joseph Smith said that the Gospel of Jesus Christ has the ability to make bad men good and good men better. Humble Latter-day Saints who are doing their best to live the Gospel will never say they're better people than their inactive or nonmember neighbor; it isn't about making comparisons. All it means is that they know how the Gospel has changed their lives, and they wish the same for you!

Christians of every stripe talk of making these changes, of being born again. Many believe all it takes is a mere confession of faith; for others, it means participation in the church's sacraments. But in a Gospel sense (we're not talking dieting here!), what does real change consist of? King Benjamin describes it best:

> *And they all cried with one voice, saying: Yea, we believe all the words which thou hast spoken unto us; and also, we know of their surety and truth, because of the Spirit of the Lord Omnipotent, which has wrought a mighty change in us, or in our hearts, that we have no more disposition to do evil, but to do good continually.* (Mosiah 5:2)

What is this mighty change? What is the result of

being born again? King Benjamin's people state it clearly, namely, "that we have no more disposition to do evil, but to do good continually." This is the mighty change that has occurred in their hearts.

The good king then explains that if they enter into a covenant with God, they can become his heirs:

And now, because of the covenant which ye have made ye shall be called the children of Christ, his sons, and his daughters; for behold, this day he hath spiritually begotten you; for ye say that your hearts are changed through faith on his name; therefore, ye are born of him and have become his sons and his daughters. (Mosiah 5:7)

His sons and his daughters? What does that mean? Elder Theodore M. Burton gives this answer:

Now, if we are born again, we must be born into a family. Into whose family are we born? Why, into the family of Jesus Christ! The scriptures refer to the Savior as the Bridegroom and to the church as the bride. Through baptism, then, we become children in that royal family, with Jesus Christ as our Father. Through the baptismal ordinance we take upon ourselves a new family name—the name of Jesus Christ. Paul states that we are thereby adopted as the sons and daughters of Jesus Christ. (Theodore M. Burton, *"To Be Born Again," Ensign,* Sept. 1985, pg. 66)

Note these words of Paul given to the Romans:

For as many as are led by the Spirit of God, they are the sons [and daughters] of God.

For ye have not received the spirit of bondage again to fear; but ye have received the Spirit of adoption, whereby we cry, Abba, Father.

The Spirit itself beareth witness with our spirit, that we are the children of God:

And if children, then heirs; heirs of God, and joint-heirs with Christ; if so be that we suffer with him [that is, if we are obedient and serve as Jesus Christ has done], that we may be also glorified together. (Rom. 8:14–17.)

The message is that God's faithful children will stand to inherit all that He has — that's what heirs do! Children inherit what their parents leave them. That is why the Gospel is called the "Good News." What news could be better than that?

In order to take advantage of the Good News, there is a price we have to pay, and that price is to "bury the old man and take up the new" — leave the BEFORE man behind in favor of the new and improved AFTER version.

Elder Burton reminds us that baptism richly symbolizes many things. He reminds us that Paul likened baptism to the crucifixion and resurrection of Jesus.

Know ye not, that so many of us as were baptized into Jesus Christ were baptized into his death?

Therefore we are buried with him by baptism into death: that like as Christ was raised up from the dead by the glory of the Father, even so we also should walk in newness of life.

For if we have been planted together in the likeness of his death, we shall be [raised out of the water] also in the likeness of his resurrection:

Knowing this, that our old man [that is, our former unrighteous life] is crucified with him, that the body of sin might be destroyed, that henceforth we should not serve sin [that is, the devil]. (Rom. 6:6 – 9)

"In other words, there must be a 'death' to the type of life most people live. The wicked self must die," Elder Burton notes.

In my own thinking, I define wickedness simply as disobedience to God. Personal disobedience, or wickedness, must cease and die. Furthermore, disobedience to the laws of God must not only die and be buried but must remain dead and buried. Such a change of life for the better is normally called repentance. All personal disobedience to God must end and be replaced by a willingness to keep his laws and his commandments.

Repentance precedes baptism, and baptism is the ordinance by which former sins are washed away. The washing in water symbolizes the purification of our soul, just as bathing in water cleanses our bodies from the grime and dirt of everyday living and makes us feel refreshed again. But baptism symbolizes something more. It is the beginning of a new life. Just as the resurrection purges the dross and imperfections of mortality and renews and perfects the body, so baptism cleanses the soul from sin and prepares a person to lead a better, more perfect life in the future. We can see how apt Paul's simile was in which he compared baptism with death and the resurrection.

This is explained in the Pearl of Great Price:

Inasmuch as ye were born into the world by water, and blood, and the spirit, which I have made, and so became of dust a living soul [the creation process], even so ye must be born again into the kingdom of heaven, of water, and of the Spirit, and be cleansed by blood, even the blood of mine Only Begotten; that ye might be sanctified from all sin, and enjoy the words of eternal life in this world, and eternal life in the world to come, even immortal glory."

For by the water ye keep the commandment; by the Spirit ye are justified, and by the blood ye are sanctified." (Moses 6:59 – 60.)

This change, Elder Burton explains, comes

By the atonement of Jesus Christ, baptism would remain just a dead form. Baptism alone cannot save us. Works alone cannot save us. Baptism must be accompanied by the granting of the Holy Ghost, which makes us spiritually alive just as God breathed into Adam the breath of life when he was created. Without the Holy Ghost, we would be spiritually stillborn and not have power to enter the presence of God the Eternal Father. (Theodore M. Burton, "To Be Born Again," *Ensign,* Sept. 1985, pg. 66)

That is one of the gifts of being born again, that sure knowledge of the power of the atonement... that life does not end at death nor begin at birth and that, with God's help, we have the power to change.

"Change is a choice," President Ezra Taft Benson, says: "When you choose to follow Christ, you choose to be changed. It is no wonder, then, that Nephi admonished his people to 'feast upon the words of Christ; for behold, the words of Christ will tell you all things what ye should do.' (2 Ne. 32:3.)"

Jesus said:

Not every one that saith unto me, Lord, Lord, shall enter into the kingdom of heaven; but he that doeth the will of my Father which is in heaven. (Matt. 7:21)

Enter ye in at the strait gate. (Matt. 7:15)

President David O. McKay noted that...

No man can sincerely resolve to apply in his daily life the teachings of Jesus of Nazareth without sensing a change in his own nature. The phrase 'born again' has a deeper significance than many people attach to it. This changed feeling may be indescribable, but it is real.

Can human hearts be changed? Why, of course! It happens every day in the great missionary work of the Church. It is one of the most widespread of Christ's modern miracles. If it hasn't happened to you—it should. (Pres. David O, McKay, *Conference Report,* April 1962, pg. 7).

What are some distinguishing characteristics of someone who is born again (or as President Benson described it, men "who are captained by Christ")?

A born-again person is swallowed up in the Lord's will (see John 5:30).

A born-again person will always do those things that please the Lord (John 8:29).

A born-again person will not only die for the Lord, but more important, he or she will live for Him.

A born-again person will show "by the pictures on their walls, the books on their shelves, the music in the air, their words and acts" that they follow Christ.

A born-again person will "stand as a witness of God at all times, and in all things, and in all places (see Mosiah 18:9).

A born-again person does make mistakes, but does not do so purposefully — he or she makes honest mistakes and then repents and seeks forgiveness.

A born-again person may stumble occasionally but will grab onto the iron rod in case of a slip or fall.

A born-again person is not alone — there are fellow travelers along the way to offer help.

A born-again person is not perfect but presses forward and endures to the end, letting Christ do His part.

To test us to see if we are pressing forward, Alma poses these questions for us to ponder:

> *And now behold, I ask of you, my brethren of the church, have ye spiritually been born of God? Have ye received his image in your countenances? Have ye experienced this mighty change in your hearts?*
>
> *Do ye exercise faith in the redemption of him who created you? Do you look forward with an eye of faith, and view this mortal body raised in immortality, and this corruption raised in incorruption, to stand before God to be judged according to the deeds which have been done in the mortal body?*

I say unto you, can you imagine to yourselves that ye hear the voice of the Lord, saying unto you, in that day: Come unto me ye blessed, for behold, your works have been the works of righteousness upon the face of the earth? (Alma 5: 14 – 16)

For all of us change IS possible. Others have done it. So can you. They can tell you how.

Chapter 9 — Apostasy & Restoration

As you consider the possibilities that full participation in the Gospel of Jesus Christ offers you — both in this life and the next — keep in mind one of the most famous passages in holy writ.

And this is life eternal life, that they might know thee, the only true God and Jesus Christ whom thou has sent. (John 17:3)

In other words, as we come to know God better, we get closer to our goal of eternal life. It is ironic, isn't it, that as we make small improvements, we begin to see more flaws in ourselves. Remember C. S. Lewis's observation?

When a man is getting better, he understands more and more clearly the evil that is still in him. When a man is getting worse, he understands his own badness less and less. (C.S. Lewis, *Mere Christianity* pg.93).

If we are moving toward the light, our path is illuminated; as we move away, things grow darker, more obscure. We call this Apostasy. Usually it is a gradual process. When a whole nation or people fall away, it is a general Apostasy. In church parlance, the Great Apostasy occurred after the apostles were killed, revelation and authority were lost and doctrines and ordinances were changed. No one was left who could act in God's name and perform the saving ordinances. Reformers dedicated their lives — and in many cases gave their lives — in the cause of truth. One such searcher of the truth was Roger Williams, at one time a Puritan minister and keen advocate for religious liberty. After his eviction from Puritan Massachusetts, he founded Providence, Rhode Island. For awhile he associated himself with an independent congregation of Baptists. And then after much study, he came to this conclusion:

> *In the poor small span of my life, I desired to have been a diligent and constant observer, and have been my self many ways engaged in city, in country, in court,in schools, in universities, in churches, in old and new England, and yet cannot in the holy presence of God bring in the result of a satisfying discovery, that either the begetting ministry of the apostles or messengers to the nations, or the feeding and nourishing ministry of pastors and teachers, according to the first institution of the Lord Jesus, are yet restored and extant.* (Roger Williams, *The Hireling Ministry*, in the *Complete Writings of Roger Williams*, 7 vols.)

Discouraged, Williams finally "told [his followers] that being himself misled, he had [misled them, and] he was now satisfied that there was none upon earth that could administer baptism [or any of the ordinances of the gospel], ... [so] he advised them therefore to forego all ... and wait for the coming of new apostles." (Elder Jeffrey R. Holland, "Prophets, Seers and Revelators, *Ensign,* Nov. 2004, pg. 6)

What Rev. Williams and other reformers dreamed of is now here for the taking: The Gospel of Jesus Christ has been restored with all its apostolic power ... the power to bind in heaven what is bound on earth, to seal husbands and wives together and children to parents.

The sad part is when it is so plainly evident to those who have been taught these principles, who have at least a taste of testimony and then "reject this glad message." This is what the Lord has to say about them:

All truth is independent in that sphere in which God has placed it, to act for itself, as all intelligence also; otherwise there is no existence.

Behold, here is the agency of man, and here is the condemnation of man; because that which was from the beginning is plainly manifest unto them, and they receive not the light.

And every man whose spirit receiveth not the alight is under condemnation. (D&C 93: 30 – 32)

We are free to act for ourselves, to accept or reject this glad message. But as the songwriter says, "they who reject this glad message shall never such happiness know."

We read in the Book of Mormon that "wickedness never was happiness." Conversely, righteousness leads to happiness. The Gospel has been called the Plan of Happiness. One prominent athlete noted that his conversion came about after he met the mission president and "wanted to have what he had." Parents often are activated after they send their sons and daughters into the mission field. They see the miraculous change in their missionaries and learn, despite the separation and the hardships, that their children are happier than they ever have been. And when they learn firsthand that active participation can change someone so close to them, they want to get in on the action. Two good brothers in my high priests quorum discovered exactly that when their sons piqued their interest. They learned firsthand how hard their sons worked to share the Gospel with people who couldn't see the forest for the trees when they realized they were just like that.

What both discovered is that such a piece of humble pie can be truly delicious. They would have never called their separation from the church and its blessings apostasy, just as my dad never considered himself a Jack Mormon. Many who choose to stay away on Sunday just think of it as a hiatus, a vacation, time better spent away from Gospel activity. But when viewed through the looking of glass of history and taking into account thousands and millions of others following the same path, it is apostasy. And the effect on generations yet unborn can be devastating.

That is one of the overarching themes of the Book of Mormon, namely, how in just a few years a people who were faithful and true strayed away, became proud and rebellious and forgot the lessons their parents taught them.

When I was a bishop. a fellow bishop in an adjoining ward had a young brother who lived near us. The younger brother had two sons who occasionally showed up to Scout activities, but other than that, the family had nothing to do with the Church. When I asked the bishop why he and his brothers had taken such different paths, he said his parents were active and faithful when he was growing up, but when his younger brother came along they had found other interests and never took him. By the time I knew the family, the third generation knew very little about the mission of the Savior, about the Restoration of the Gospel and Priesthood power and what was required of them to inherit Gospel blessings. Whose fault is that?

The Doctrine and Covenants spells it out clearly:

And again, inasmuch as parents have children in Zion, or in any of her stakes which are organized, that teach them not to understand the doctrine of repentance, faith in Christ the Son of the living God, and of baptism and the gift of the Holy Ghost by the laying on of the hands, when eight years old, the sin be upon the heads of the parents.

For this shall be a law unto the inhabitants of Zion, or in any of her stakes which are organized.

And their children shall be baptized for the remission of their sins when eight years old, and receive the laying on of the hands.

And they shall also teach their children to pray, and to walk uprightly before the Lord. (D&C 68: 24 – 28)

It's been my experience that while many fathers who don't know the Gospel are not so concerned about themselves, they want to make sure their children have a knowledge of God and learn right from wrong. They seem to say, "I don't need it, but I want my kids to have it." The magic happens, however, when a child pleads with a father to take their mom and the family to the temple, or when a missionary writes from home about the miracles he or she has seen take place in the lives of others. It reminds me of Lehi's vision when family members partake of the fruit of the tree and beckon others farther down the trail to grab hold of the rod and, despite the taunts of the wicked and the mists of darkness, come and join them.

This is the call Peter made after the death of Christ to those who had initially rejected the Savior's message as recorded in Acts:

Repent ye therefore, and be converted , that your sins may be blotted out, when the times of refreshing shall come from the presence of the Lord;

And he shall send Jesus Christ, which before was preached unto you:

Whom the heaven must receive until the times of restitution of all things, which God hath spoken by the mouth of all his holy prophets since the world began. (Acts 3:19–21)

The times of restitution Peter referred to are now when the Restored Gospel is on the earth for the last time. As the folk singer put it, "the times they are a changing..." Never before have people needed the

Gospel message more than they do now. Satan rages, terrorists kill for the pleasure of it, lust and greed are the trade of the day. Nearly all parents want to keep their children far away and safe from sin. But the only true way to do that is to take the Straight and Narrow Path and lead the way. As I experienced in my dream as a boy, a child requires a parent to sit in the driver's seat. The Gospel has been restored, it is there for the taking for those who are seeking the truth. Millions testify that the Great Apostasy, for them at least, has ended. Listen to what they have to say.

Chapter 10 — Testimony & Witnesses

There is an ancient law handed down from the time of Moses that plays a part in jurisprudence in every court in every land. It is the law of witnesses. Paul reminds the Corinthians that

In the mouth of two or three witnesses shall every word be established. (II Cor. 13:1)

That's why once a month in every LDS ward and branch all over the world fast and testimony meetings are held. Anyone with the inclination may stand and bear witness. Some testimonies are the simple expressions of faith of a small child, others are the heartfelt admissions of trials and forgiveness of a member bowed down by the burdens of life. They all serve a purpose.

The message is: If you don't have a testimony, you can get one. It costs no money, but there is a price. As Joseph Smith explains in his own history, he went into the woods to pray after reading the Epistle of James who promised that, "if any of you lack wisdom, let him ask of

God, that giveth to all men liberally and upbraideth him not; and it shall be given him. (James 1:5) In other words, God won't hold it against you if you ask: He wants you to. The new subtitle to the Book or Mormon emphasizes the importance of additional witnesses. It says: Another Testament of Jesus Christ (in addition to the Old Testament and the New Testament). The scriptures remind us that testimonies of God are all around us, in nature, in the inner workings of atoms, in the movement of heavenly bodies and in the smile of a child. They are there for all those who have eyes to see.

And there are different testimonies to be had: a testimony that God lives, that Jesus is the Christ, that the Book of Mormon is true, that Joseph Smith was a prophet of God, that the Priesthood has been restored and that families can be together forever. One testimony leads to another. Often, however, people stub their toes on a stumbling block, and rather than moving from testimony to testimony, from a a flicker of light to great illumination, the testimony grows dim until it fades out. That's why it's so important to remember how we got it in the first place, and how we can renew it year after year.

The Book of Mormon has been called the keystone of our religion because it ties everything together: the testimony of Christ's mission from the New Testament with the message of the Restoration and advent of a new dispensation with the keys of heaven returned to earth for the last time. That's why the Book of Mormon is so important and why the testimony of Moroni is so essential for those seeking the truth:

> *And when ye shall receive these things, I would exhort you that ye would ask God, the Eternal Father, in the name of Christ, if these things are not true; and if ye shall ask with a sincere heart, with real intent, having faith in Christ, he will manifest the truth of it unto you, by the power of the Holy Ghost.*
>
> *And by the power of the Holy Ghost ye may know the truth of all things.* (Moroni 10: 4 – 5)

That is either a powerful promise given by an ancient prophet of God or a cynical verse inserted by a deceiver for his own gain. But what could Joseph Smith — if he were set on deception — gain by inserting such verses? Nothing! For if the book were false, a true God would not add his testimony; and if there were no God, neither would there come a confirmation.

There is only one way to find out: read the book and pray about it. Millions testify to its truthfulness. Joseph Smith himself left his own testimony about his calling and about his translation of Mormon's record.

It is a powerful testimony in and of itself:

It caused me serious reflection then, and often has since, how very strange it was that an obscure boy, of a little over fourteen years of age , and one, too, who was doomed to the necessity of obtaining a scanty maintenance by his daily labor , should be thought a character of sufficient importance to attract the attention of the great ones of the most popular sects of the day, and in a manner to create in them a spirit of the most bitter cpersecution and reviling . But strange or not, so it was, and it was often the cause of great sorrow to myself.

However, it was nevertheless a fact that I had beheld a vision. I have thought since, that I felt much like Paul, when he made his defense before King Agrippa, and related the account of the vision he had when he saw a light, and heard a voice; but still there were but few who believed him; some said he was dishonest, others said he was mad; and he was ridiculed and reviled. But all this did not destroy the reality of his vision. He had seen a vision, he knew he had, and all the persecution under heaven could not make it otherwise; and though they should persecute him unto death, yet he knew, and would know to his latest breath, that he had both seen a light and heard a voice speaking unto him, and all the world could not make him think or believe otherwise.

So it was with me. I had actually seen a light, and in the midst of that light I saw two Personages, and they did in reality speak to me; and though I was hated and persecuted for saying that I had seen a vision, yet it was true; and while they were persecuting me, reviling me, and speaking all manner of evil against me falsely for so saying, I was led to say in my heart: Why persecute me for telling the truth? I have actually seen a vision; and who am I that I can withstand God, or why does the world think to make me deny what I have actually seen? For I had seen a vision; I knew it, and I knew that God knew it, and I could not deny it, neither dared I do it; at least I knew that by so doing I would offend God, and come under condemnation.

I had now got my mind satisfied so far as the sectarian world was concerned—that it was not my duty to join with any of them, but to continue as I was until further directed. I had found the testimony of James to be true—that a man who lacked wisdom might ask of God, and obtain, and not be upbraided. (Pearl of Great Price, Joseph Smith History 23 – 26)

This frontier farmboy's testimony is simple and straightforward, that what James promised is, in fact, true, that God does hear and answer prayers. That is the essence of the message of the restoration. And it is a testimony you can have!

As I said, it costs nothing, but there may be a price, as my seminary teacher John Heidenreich discovered.

President Gordon B. Hinckley related the story of a young military officer from a non-Christian nation who met Church members while on a military training mission in the United States. After studying and hearing the missionary lessons, he joined the Church. When President Hinckley met him, he asked him if he were worried about his career and livelihood when his superiors discovered he had joined the Church. His reply to the president was sobering: "It's true, isn't it? Then, that's all that matters."

It IS true. That is the secret of the success of the Church of Jesus Christ of Latter-day Saints. It is the Spirit of the Holy Ghost working in the lives of millions of members, testifying to them that their course in life is correct, that they are on the path to eternal life. Weekly, faithful members partake of the sacrament to renew their covenant to get their weekly dose of testimony to keep them strong. Consider the promise given in the sacrament prayer:

O God, the Eternal Father, we ask thee in the name of thy Son, Jesus Christ, to bless and sanctify this bread to the souls of all those who partake of it, that they may eat in remembrance of the body of thy Son, and witness unto thee,

O God, the Eternal Father, that they are willing to take upon them the name of thy Son, and always remember him and keep his commandments which he has given them; that they may always have his Spirit to be with them. Amen. (D&C 20:77)

The promise to "always have his Spirit to be with them" is the promise of a living testimony. That's the main reason to attend church, to have this promise renewed each week, to cope with the trials and tragedies of life, to withstand the blows of the Evil One, to have the ammunition to fight the good fight, not just for ourselves but also for our wives, our families, our children.

All through the scriptures, witness is borne of the veracity of the work. The Lord himself promises that those who accept the testimony of the Book of Mormon will be "born of him."

And in addition to your testimony, the testimony of three of my servants, whom I shall call and ordain, unto whom I will show these things, and they shall go forth with my words that are given through you.

Yea, they shall know of a surety that these things are true, for from heaven will I declare it unto them.

I will give them power that they may behold and view these things as they are;

And to none else will I grant this power, to receive this same testimony among this generation, in this the beginning of the rising up and the coming forth of my church out of the wilderness —clear as the moon, and fair as the sun, and terrible as an army with banners.

And the testimony of three witnesses will I send forth of my word.

And behold, whosoever believeth on my words, them will I visit with the manifestation of my Spirit; and they shall be born of me, even of water and of the Spirit. (D&C 5:11–16)

Shortly after Joseph Smith received this revelation in March of 1829, his great burden of carrying the testimony of the record and the golden plates was then shared with first the three witnesses, and then the eight witnesses. The Lord made sure that the ancient law of witnesses was upheld when Oliver Cowdery, David Whitmer and Martin Harris were privileged to see the Angel Moroni and see the plates and hear the voice of the Lord. Their witness and the witness of the other eight are recorded in the front of the Book of Mormon:

And we also testify that we have seen the engravings which are upon the plates; and they have been shown unto us by the power of God, and not of man. And we declare with words of soberness, that an angel of God came down from heaven, and he brought and laid before our eyes, that we beheld and saw the plates, and the engravings thereon; and we know that it is by the grace of God the Father, and our Lord Jesus Christ, that we beheld and bear record that these things are true. And it is marvelous in our eyes. Nevertheless, the voice of the Lord commanded us that we should bear record of it; wherefore, to be obedient unto the commandments of God, we bear testimony of these things.

It is one thing to have an understanding of the principles of the Gospel and of the programs of the Church. It is possible to admire what the church does for the family, the poor and needy and ancestors long gone thanks to the Church family history program. Certainly, even cynics can appreciate what the Church does for its members and for others in need.

But that is not enough.

An understanding, an appreciation and even a knowledge of the Church and its message are not enough: What is required is a testimony.

During his ministry, Christ taught his disciples the Gospel, performed miracles and showed the way. But a real understanding of who He really was and the purpose of His ministry didn't come to Peter and the other apostles until the Day of Pentecost when the promised arrival of the Holy Ghost took place.

But Peter, standing up with the eleven, lifted up his voice, and said unto them, Ye men of Judaea, and all ye that dwell at Jerusalem, be this known unto you, and hearken to my words:

For these are not drunken, as ye suppose, seeing it is but the third hour of the day.

But this is that which was spoken by the prophet Joel;

And it shall come to pass in the last days, saith God, I will pour out of my Spirit upon all flesh: and your sons and your daughters shall prophesy, and your young men shall see visions, and your old men shall dream dreams:

And on my servants and on my handmaidens I will pour out in those days of my Spirit; and they shall prophesy. (Acts 2: 14 – 18)

That power is again on the earth, the power to see visions and dream dreams. It is the stuff of which testimonies are made, the simple testimonies of the small child and the powerful witness of a gray-haired prophet.

It is a sure witness, a still, small voice, the peace of assurance that all is well, even when the world is upside down and all is in turmoil.

Your testimony is there for the asking. It requires, as Alma said, first a desire to believe that we let work in us. It demands effort on our part: study, prayer and church attendance. And as the dawn of this new day approaches, it requires a broken heart and a contrite spirit, the humility to change when change is required. Then, line upon line, precept upon precept, it comes like dew on fresh grass, imperceptible at first, then pours in when we let it.

I knew at a young age that Joseph Smith was a prophet. It was when I preparing a talk in stake conference that my inactive dad typed for me. I don't know why I was asked to give the talk, me, the son of a Jack Mormon. But Jack typed it for me, helping me to properly pronounce the words "urim and thummim" (the instruments the Prophet used to translate the plates). Since that time, when I hear the song "Oh How Lovely Was the Morning" I get a lump in my throat and tears in my eyes. That is a testimony.

Since then, my testimony has grown to a certain knowledge that Joseph's prayer was answered, that the Father and the Son did appear to him in that grove of trees in 1820, that the Book of Mormon is indeed the story of a fallen people and a lesson for us today and that Priesthood power is again on the earth and that families can be sealed together in the temple of the Lord for time and all eternity.

I am no one special. But I have an angel for a wife, seven bright, beautiful children, and, so far, six gifted grandchildren. My mother stayed true and faithful and waited for her husband to decide that he wanted the Gospel blessings for his family. I watched him make those tough changes. I know how hard it was, but I learned it is possible. I pray that all my posterity will grab on to the iron rod and stay on the Straight and Narrow path and partake of the fruit that father Lehi saw in his dream.

That is my wish for my family.

And for yours.